FIRST TIME INVESTOR

Your Guide to Investing in the Australian Stock Market

JOHN ENGLISH

DoctorZed
Publishing
www.doctorzed.com

Copies of this book can be ordered via booksellers or by contacting:

DoctorZed Publishing
10 Vista Ave, Skye,
South Australia 5072
www.doctorzed.com

ISBN: 978-0-6455705-3-3 (hc)
ISBN: 978-0-6455705-4-0 (sc)
ISBN: 978-0-6455705-5-7 (e)

First edition 2022

A CiP number is available at the National Library of Australia.

Because of the dynamic nature of the Internet, any web addresses or links contained in this book may have changed since publication and may no longer be valid. The views expressed in this work are solely those of the author and do not necessarily reflect the views of the publisher, and the publisher hereby disclaims any responsibility for them.

Cover image © Rawpixelimages | Dreamstime.com

DoctorZed Publishing rev. date: 21/09/2022

CONTENTS

FIGURES

PREFACE

This book is written for the do-it-yourself investor. Its purpose is to equip you with the information you need to take control of your own investment decisions. It is not a get-rich-quick book, nor is it a theoretical textbook. It is a practical book that is written for people who want to invest in the Australian stockmarket.

If you are interested in investing and not sure where to begin, this book will get you started. If you are ready to make your first investment, this book will answer your questions and aid you in making informed decisions. If you have already taken the plunge, this book will sharpen your investment skills and your capacity to evaluate recommendations from stockbrokers and other financial advisers.

- Part A is focused on the first steps toward becoming an investor. It explains how to prepare yourself to become an investor, how to buy and sell on the Australian stockmarket, and how to find investment information.

- Part B is about starting out in shares. It describes the features of ordinary and preference shares, risk and return in shares, how to look for value in shares, and how to use technical trading systems.

- Part C is about starting out in managed investments. It describes the pros and cons of managed investments, various types of managed funds in Australia, the impact of fees, and the track record for actively managed funds.

- Part D is about options and futures. It explains exchange traded share options, low exercise price options, warrants, index options, index futures, and interest rate futures.
- Part E is about fixed income investments. It describes the role of fixed income investments, the features of fixed income investments, risk and return in fixed income investments, and strategies for trading fixed income investments.

The language of investing is part of the unique excitement of the stockmarket. It is intentionally colourful, sometimes dramatic, and occasionally looks like a secret code. Learning the language is an important part of becoming an investor. When specialised financial terms are first used, they appear in italics. Whenever you want to refresh your understanding of them, you can refer to the glossary at the end of the book.

John English was a stockbroker and floor trader on the New York Stock Exchange before coming to Australia to take up an academic career. He was Deputy Director of the Australian Innovation Research Centre and Associate Professor of Finance and Entrepreneurship at the University of Tasmania. *First Time Investor* is the product of a lifetime of active trading, university teaching, and investment research. His unique blend of professional training and practical experience makes this book essential reading for every new investor.

Part A

BECOMING
AN INVESTOR

The notion that the stockmarket is restricted to wealthy individuals is a myth. Millions of individuals with relatively modest means are the backbone of Australian investing. The number of Australian investors is accelerating, including a surprise upswing during the Pandemic as a new wave of investors entered the market. If you are new to investing, then it is natural that you will have a lot of questions.

Part A is designed to overcome the concerns that all new investors experience. It explains how to prepare yourself to become an investor, how to buy and sell on the Australian stockmarket, and how to find investment information.

CHAPTER 1

DECIDING TO TAKE THE PLUNGE

There is more to investing than simply throwing money at something and following what happens to it. Becoming an investor begins by finding answers to some important questions.

- Am I ready to start investing?
- What goals do I want to achieve?
- What level of risk am I prepared to accept?
- What will be my investment strategy?
- What are the key investment decisions I need to make?

AM I READY TO START INVESTING?

For most individuals holding a job, saving money, and buying a home are a means of achieving financial security. The decision to become an investor is also motivated by a desire for financial well-being into the future. There is a first time for everything, and investing is no different. Here are a few things to consider before you take the plunge.

- Be sure you can meet all of your normal living expenses and obligations before you invest.
- Have investment goals that are consistent with your knowledge, ability, financial position, and your emotional tolerance for risk.

- Realise that you cannot predict the future, but you can be sensitive to changing conditions that affect your investments.

- Be willing to take your losses when you are wrong without fear and without feeling guilty. Do not expect a miracle to bail you out of a declining stock or to put you onto a winner.

- Give special thought to long-term investing. It is usually more suitable for first time investors or individuals who might be susceptible to excessive gloom or optimism.

- If you have enough capital and an urge to speculate, then go ahead and give in to it a little. But do it intelligently with only a small part of your funds. A loss may cure your speculative itch forever.

How much time and effort are you willing to devote to your investments? At one extreme is a passive approach in which you are not interested in spending too much time or effort in managing your investments. At the other extreme is an active approach in which you are intimately involved with every detail of your investment program.

A *passive* approach to investing consists of buying good quality investments with no particular view about selling them in the future. The biggest advantage of passive investing is its simplicity. It also discourages inexperienced investors from needlessly or repeatedly changing their investments. The disadvantage is that a passive buy-and-hold policy simply fails to manage the investments. Under-performing investments are not replaced, profits are not harvested, and the mix of investments may drift away from what was originally intended. An alternative to passive investing is to invest in a managed fund and let a professional investment manager make the decisions for you.

An *active* approach to investing consists of changing the exposure to different investments to take advantage of emerging opportunities. If you increase an exposure beyond its usual allocation, then your portfolio is *overweight* in that investment. If the exposure is less than its usual allocation, then it is *underweight* in that investment. An active approach to investing means continuously adjusting your investments to match your outlook for the economy, various industry sectors and individual companies. If your skill and judgement are good, then you could earn higher rewards than with passive investing. If your choices turn out to be poor, then active investing is more likely to produce losses.

WHAT ARE MY GOALS?

There are two reasons why people invest. The first reason is to accumulate wealth. The second reason is to derive an income from the wealth that has been accumulated. Most individuals spend their entire working life trying to accumulate wealth. They may not recognise this as an investment goal, but it is nevertheless their primary financial objective. Undertaking a genuine investment program, however, requires goals that are more specific. What do you want to achieve by investing? Are you putting money away for your children's education? Are you building a nest egg for your retirement? Do you want to experience the excitement of speculating? Your investment goals will necessarily be tempered by your financial position, your age, your tax position, and the amount of risk you are willing to bear.

- A sound financial position and adequate income are important prerequisites for becoming an investor. Do you have ample provision for normal living expenses, some savings for emergencies, moderate debts, and adequate life insurance?

- Your age is perhaps the next consideration in determining your investment goals. While there are no hard and fast rules, generally from the 20s through the 40s the main objective is growth. During the 50s growth is still significant but income becomes increasingly important. From the 60's onward retirement income and avoiding risk are most important.

- Tax effectiveness will also be an important factor in shaping your investment program. The prospect of tax avoidance, however, should not be allowed to distort good investment judgement.

- Your attitude towards risk should also be reflected in your investment goals. You assume some risk simply by deciding to be an investor. The question is how much uncertainty and possibility of loss can you withstand before you exceed your threshold for risk?

When you are clear about your individual circumstances, you are in a position to translate this information into investment goals. The objective is to establish the relative importance of three things – growth, income, and risk.

- Growth is important to people who are trying to accumulate wealth. There are different ways in which to pursue a growth-oriented investment program. One growth investor may follow a speculative growth strategy while another may prefer long-term investments in high quality stocks.

6

- The amount and stability of income is important for individuals who want to live on their investments. The emphasis may be on fixed income investments or shares with regular dividends.

- Avoiding risk is an important goal for everyone, but its importance varies according to your circumstances and your investment temperament. It means more than simply guarding the value of your investments. It also means protecting the purchasing power of your money against inflation.

If your primary goal is growth, then you want investments that are likely to increase in value so they may be sold for more than their initial cost. If your primary goal is income, then you want investments that provide interest or dividend payments regularly and dependably. If, however, your primary goal is to avoid risk, then you want investments that offer the greatest safety of principal and protection from inflation. Unfortunately, there is no single investment that simultaneously offers maximum growth, maximum income, and minimum risk. These three investment goals are like the corners of a triangle. The closer you move towards one corner, the further you move away from the others.

WHAT IS MY TOLERANCE FOR RISK?

The trade-off between risk and return is the foundation for establishing investment goals. The obvious risk in investing is the chance that you may lose money. If you are looking for higher returns, then you will accept greater risk. If you are not a big risk-taker, then you should be willing to accept lower returns.

Inasmuch as no one knows for sure what the future holds, investors face varying degrees of uncertainty about the returns from individual investments. Most people do not like to take risks, and they can only be enticed to do so by the potential for greater returns. However, everyone varies in their degree of risk aversion ranging from being a conservative investor to being a speculative investor. The important point is that each of us has a different attitude toward taking risks and recognising our attitude is vital in determining our investment goals. Let's examine your attitude towards risk. Suppose you have $100,000 to invest and you can choose one of the following three investments.

Investment one: You can deposit your money in the bank for one year at a fixed interest rate of 4 percent per annum. There is no uncertainty about the bank's ability to pay and you know that in one year you will get $4,000 in interest plus the return of your $100,000 principal irrespective of changes in interest rates or price movements in the stock market.

Investment two: You can invest your money for one year in a portfolio of ordinary shares in large, established companies with good records of earnings and dividends. You know that the combination of dividends and capital gains can vary according to the state of the economy and the performance of each of the individual companies. If things go badly, you might lose $25,000. If things go well, you might gain $25,000. You expect the most likely outcome will be a return of about $10,000.

Investment three: You can put your money into the shares of a new high-technology company that is developing a promising new process using lasers. It is still in the research and development stage and the extent of the market for its products is not yet clear. If the company fails, you will lose your entire investment. If the company is successful, your investment could easily be worth $500,000 at the end of a year.

How do you feel about the bank deposit? If a $4,000 return is satisfactory and you do not want to take any chances with your principal, then this may be the right investment for you. What about the portfolio of ordinary shares? If the possibility of higher returns outweighs the possibility of a moderate loss, then this may represent the right investment for you. If you are prepared to accept much greater risk in an attempt to gain very large returns, then the high-technology company may offer you the right trade-off between risk and return. Or does the all-or-nothing nature of this investment make you apprehensive? If you are not prepared to live with this much uncertainty, then it is probably because it exceeds your tolerance for risk.

The level of risk that matters most is the one you can live with when the market is sinking to new lows. Most investors are naturally optimistic at the top of a bull market and pessimistic at the bottom of a bear market. However, the big returns from stockmarket investing are based on buying when the market is at a low and selling when the market is at a high. Many investors were severely tested, for example, during the market crash at the start of the Pandemic in 2020.

WHAT IS MY INVESTMENT STRATEGY?

An investment strategy is designed to achieve an investment goal. Investment strategies consist of growth strategies, income strategies, balanced strategies, and speculative strategies.

Growth strategy

The goal of a growth investment strategy is to realise significant capital gains over the medium to longer-term. Income is not important. The way in which growth is pursued, however, depends upon the amount of risk an investor is willing to accept. A growth investment strategy usually focuses on ordinary shares of varying quality. It is not unusual for a growth portfolio to experience periods of significant volatility.

Investment decisions in a growth portfolio are generally based on an attempt to predict short to medium-term market fluctuations. A growth investor needs to be prepared to completely change their investments to protect the portfolio against short-term risk or to take advantage of a change in the investment environment. Growth portfolios typically maintain some cash reserves to take advantage of new opportunities. A growth portfolio can achieve superior returns if the investor correctly predicts the market's reaction to events and takes advantage of developing trends. A growth portfolio can result in large losses, however, if the investor gets into a whipsawing market or if their predictions are wrong.

Income strategy

The goal of an income investment strategy is safety of principal, a good yield, and enough growth to offset inflation. Income strategies may focus on higher-grade fixed income securities, preference shares, and good quality ordinary shares that reliably pay fully franked dividends.

Investments in an income strategy are relatively constant. It is unlikely that they would be altered in reaction to temporary market moves. After significant market shifts, however, the portfolio may need to be readjusted. For example, if shares increase relative to fixed income securities, then readjusting would consist of selling some of the lower-yielding shares and using the proceeds to buy higher-yielding fixed interest securities. Most income strategies are fully invested with little cash reserves. An income strategy performs best when the investment environment is stable. It may lose ground in a strongly trending market or in the initial stages of a fundamental change in the economy.

Balanced strategy

The goal of a balanced investment strategy is stability, an average income, and enough capital gains to offset inflation and achieve moderate long-term growth. A balanced investment strategy generally includes quality ordinary shares, preference shares and fixed income securities.

A balanced investment strategy ignores short-term market movements and is focused on longer-term trends. Changes to the portfolio are based on an assessment of the relative value of shares and fixed income securities. Over a full investment cycle, the portfolio weighting between them may alter significantly. Balanced investment strategies usually include some modest cash reserves. A balanced investment strategy has the potential to avoid major downturns because of the emphasis on the relative value of shares versus fixed income securities. It performs well in a rising market because it is realising capital gains and reinvesting the proceeds. It may under-perform, however, during a prolonged period of price decline.

Speculation

The goal of a speculative strategy is maximum capital gains, with the least amount of invested capital, in the shortest period of time. A speculator is willing to accept high levels of risk and they have little concern for income, current business conditions, or long-term trends. At different times, a speculative portfolio may have leveraged positions in shares, rights, warrants, options, or futures contracts. A speculator will probably pursue concentration as opposed to diversification and they may be fully invested on some occasions and completely out of the market on others. The fact is there are very few individuals who are genuine speculators. Most people have more conservative objectives and if they decide to speculate, they do it with only a small part of their capital. Ordinary investors simply cannot afford the time and effort that goes into managing a speculative investment strategy.

HOW WILL I INVEST MY MONEY?

Having a clear investment strategy puts you in a position to make the key decisions about how you will invest your money. When you feel confident about making these decisions, you are ready to become an investor.

Asset allocation

Asset allocation refers to the proportion of investments you decide to hold in different asset classes such as cash, fixed income securities, and shares. Figure 1.1 illustrates hypothetical asset allocations for different investment strategies. The income strategy has 80 percent of its funds in cash and fixed income securities with only 20 percent in shares. The balanced strategy has 50 percent in cash and fixed income securities balanced by 50 percent in shares. The growth strategy is 80 percent in shares and 20 percent in cash and fixed income securities. The speculative strategy consists entirely of shares. Asset allocation decisions are not permanent. As your investment goals change, your asset allocations will change as well.

Figure 1.1 Asset allocation (all percent)

Investment Strategy	Cash	Fixed Income Securities	Shares
Income	15	65	20
Balanced	10	40	50
Growth	5	15	80
Speculative			100

Timing

Asset allocation also depends on economic and market conditions at the time you are making your investment decisions. As the economy moves from expansion to recession and back again, each asset class reacts differently.

For example, you might be more interested in shares when the economy is growing vigorously and then switch to fixed income securities when the economy is sliding into recession. This ebb and flow of the economic tide is commonly called the *business cycle*. Indicators such as gross domestic product, interest rates, employment, and consumer spending are used to assess changes in the business cycle.

Selection

Selection is the process of identifying individual investments within each asset class. You can simplify the process of selection by using decision rules. Decision rules consist of establishing criteria for accepting or rejecting individual investments. They may be based on fundamental analysis, technical analysis, or other types of benchmarks. The process of specifying decision rules is useful because it causes you to think about what kind of investments you want. Decision rules reduce the search time and the cost of finding suitable investment candidates by acting as a filter. *Stock screeners* are an excellent tool for applying decision rules to selection. Decision rules differ enormously from one investor to another depending on the investment strategy each has chosen and the amount of risk they are prepared to accept.

Diversification

Diversification affords protection against near catastrophic loss if the market turns against any one of your investments. This is important because many investors are under-diversified. Diversification is not just a matter of dividing your investment dollars amongst different investments. The key to diversification is to have a combination of investments in which each is affected differently by changing economic and financial market conditions. The result is that the ups and downs for various investments tend to offset each other. Examples of diversification techniques include investing in managed funds, investing across a range of industry sectors, investing across a range of asset classes, and mixing in some international investments.

Concentration is the flip side of diversification. It calls for limiting the number of investments to only a few that are carefully selected. Clearly, this is putting all your eggs in one basket. If you are correct, you will reap the benefits. If you are not, you will suffer losses. Diversification versus concentration is important in the risk-return trade-off. For most investors, the prudent approach is some form of selective diversification.

Liquidity

Market liquidity and cash reserves are an important ingredient in your investment strategy. Market liquidity refers to selecting securities with sufficient trading volume to enable buying and selling to take place easily and at a realistic price. Without market liquidity, you may have difficulty finding a buyer or seller willing to trade at an acceptable price. Market liquidity is generally greatest in the shares of the top 50 companies compared to the shares of smaller companies that may not trade for days.

Having some cash in reserve enables you to take advantage of sudden price breaks or new opportunities. Cash reserves are usually kept in the form of a bank account or very liquid fixed income securities. Cash reserves can be set aside from interest payments, dividends, or the periodic sale of some of your investments. The amount that you decide to keep in cash reserves not only depends upon the investment environment, but also on your investment goals.

Monitoring results

Once you start investing, you will need to monitor the results. Regularly evaluating the performance of each investment in your portfolio will show you where you got it right and where you did not. This will not only help you make better investment decisions in the future, but it will also identify parts of your portfolio that may need to be changed.

The objective is to determine which investments you want to continue to hold, which investments you want to increase, and which investments need to be sold. One method is to rank your investments according to their performance. Then ask yourself, 'Why should I continue to hold an investment that I would not be prepared to buy today?'

If your portfolio has been constructed for growth, then slow-moving investments should be replaced by ones with better prospects for capital gains. If income is your goal, then investments with low or falling yields should be replaced with ones that have better yields. If stability and safety are your most important considerations, then high-risk investments with roller-coaster price volatility should be replaced with investments that are more reliable.

SUMMARY

Becoming an investor consists of finding answers to some important questions before you take the plunge. Are you ready to start investing? Why do you want to invest and what are the goals you want to achieve? What risks you are prepared to take and what risks do you want to avoid? What will be the overall investment strategy for achieving your investment goals? What will be your guidelines for asset allocation, investment timing, asset selection, diversification, liquidity, and monitoring the results?

CHAPTER 2

HOW TO BUY AND SELL

The objective of this chapter is to explain the process of buying and selling on the Australian stockmarket. It begins by introducing the four main categories of investments. The central features of the chapter deal with choosing a stockbroker, opening an account, placing an order, and how settlement and transfer of ownership takes place. The chapter concludes with a discussion about borrowing money to invest.

TYPES OF INVESTMENTS

The word *investment* is a general term that includes a variety of financial instruments. They consist of shares, managed investments, options and futures, and fixed income investments. Each represents a different form of investment, and each has its own risk and return characteristics.

Shares

Investors in shares are owners, and every public company must issue ordinary shares. A company may also issue other types of shares, such as preference shares and partly paid or contributing shares, and each differs according to the rights and benefits they confer upon the shareholder. Historically, shares have performed best for growth and protection against inflation. They offer potential for capital gains and dividend income if the company is successful. The average annual return on Australian shares has been 9.7 percent over the thirty years up to the 30th of June 2021. An investment of $10,000 in shares would have grown to $160,498 in that time. Shares are also susceptible to fluctuations in market price, and investors may suffer losses if the market crashes, as it did at the beginning of the Pandemic or if an individual company experiences misfortune.

Managed investments

Managed investments are an arrangement in which individual investor funds are combined into one portfolio that is managed by a fund manager. Managed investments are particularly attractive to small investors because they offer diversification and professional investment management. Some managed investments are listed on a securities exchange and others are bought and sold directly through the fund manager. Some are actively managed seeking maximum returns and others are passively managed seeking minimum risk.

Options and futures

Options and futures contracts represent a claim on another asset. Changes in the value of options and futures flow directly from changes in the value of the underlying asset. They can be used to speculate in the underlying asset or to hedge against price changes in the underlying asset. Options and futures also offer a high degree of leverage. They consist of share options, low exercise price options, warrants, index options, index futures and interest rate futures.

Fixed income investments

Investors in fixed income investments are lenders and, therefore, creditors. Fixed income investments are issued by the Commonwealth government, state governments and companies.

They include bonds, debentures, and notes. They promise to pay a fixed amount of interest on specific dates and to repay the principal amount on a maturity date. They may be long-term such as twenty years or short-term such as thirty days. Secured fixed income investments are backed by the issuer's property, while investors in unsecured fixed income investments rely on the general credit standing of the issuer. They are generally considered a safer investment than shares because the issuer promises to repay the full amount at maturity and the interest payments are usually fixed and secure so long as the issuer remains solvent. The average annual return from Australian bonds has been 7.0 percent over the thirty years to 30 June 2021. An investment of $10,000 in Australian bonds would have grown to $75,807 in that time. However, the unprecedented low interest rates in recent times have had a significant impact on returns from fixed income investments.

CHOOSING A STOCKBROKER

A stockbroker is a firm that is licensed to buy and sell securities for the public. They charge a fee for this service called a *brokerage commission*. Stockbrokers differ in the services they offer and the fees they charge. At one end of the spectrum are full-service stockbrokers, who provide information and advice as well as handling your orders. At the other end of the spectrum are online stockbrokers who dominate the market for private investors. They depend on volume to make money and they simply take your order and do not offer advice. In between, are some new players called *robo advisors*. A listing of online and full-service stockbrokers can be found on the Australian Securities Exchange (ASX) website at ***asx.com.au***.

Online stockbroker

These are stockbrokers that only offer their services online. They simply take orders and do not offer advice. As a result, online commission rates are usually the lowest. Online trading is dominated by the big four banks including Commonwealth Bank's CommSec, National Australia Bank's Nabtrade, Westpac Bank's Westpac Online Investing, and Australia and New Zealand Banking Group's ANZ Share Investing. There is also a range of stand-alone online stockbroker websites. The number of online traders has grown significantly from around 700,000 at the end of 2019 to about 1.2 million at the end of 2021. The increase is largely attributed to new investors who came into the market during the rebound after the Pandemic crash. An online stockbroker typically appeals to the do-it-yourself investor. Here are some things to look for in an online stockbroker's website.

- What are the brokerage fees and any discounts for frequent traders?
- In addition to ASX listed shares, is access available for other securities such as options, futures, and managed investments?
- What trading tools are available such as real time market data, charting features or portfolio tracking routines?
- What research does the stockbroker's website provide including news services, ASX announcements and company profiles?
- How does their trading account operate including the procedures for placing orders, confirming orders and processing orders?
- What type of cash account is required to settle trades?

Full-service stockbroker

The role of a full-service stockbroker is different from an online stockbroker. Some full-service stockbrokers deal in nearly all types of securities, some specialise in securities of certain kinds. Some prefer to concentrate on larger clients while others base their business on small and medium size clients. The public face of the full-service stockbroker is the *client adviser*, or the firm's representative. They provide the liaison between the client and the investment services offered by the firm. Client advisers are subject to an examination of their past career and their knowledge of investments before they can be licensed to give advice and accept orders from the public. Finding a client adviser that suits your needs is a very personal decision, comparable to choosing a doctor, an accountant, or a solicitor. Full-service stockbrokers typically charge higher brokerage commissions than online stockbrokers, with some preferring to charge separately for each of the services they provide, and they can charge different rates to different clients. Full-service stockbrokers sometimes offer optional online facilities as well. Here are some things to look for in a full-service stockbroker and client adviser:

- Courteous attitude and quality service
- Ease of communications
- Efficient execution of orders
- Amount of brokerage fees
- Research and investment advice
- Margin lending facilities
- Fixed interest advice and dealing
- Portfolio management services
- Access to floats, managed investments, derivatives, and foreign securities

Robo advisor

The financial technology industry, known as *fintech*, has recently introduced automated advice services known as *robo advisors*. They are online platforms designed to do part of the job of a full-service advisor but at a lower cost and improved efficiency. They use computer algorithms and computer models to match a client's risk profile with an asset allocation recommendation. The client answers questions about things like their income, age, risk profile and how much they want to invest. The computer uses this information to recommend an allocation of the client's funds into asset classes that align with their goals.

If a client decides to proceed, the online platform will complete the transaction which is typically focused on Exchange Traded Funds (ETFs). For some first time investors it is a cost-effective way to get limited investment advice and packaged investments. Robo advisors are regulated by the ASIC and must have a financial services license.

For all the sophistication of their complex algorithms, robo advisors are no more able to guarantee a result than a human advisor. They are still subject to unexpected market swings and potential portfolio underperformance. If you need a professional client advisor at the other end of the phone, then a full-service stockbroker will be a better fit. If you prefer to choose your own investments, then an online stockbroker platform will give you greater scope and flexibility. If you think robo advice may work for you, then check out a few platforms like Stockspot, SixPark, InvestSMART, and QuietGrowth.

OPENING AN ACCOUNT

Before a stockbroker can accept an order, you need to open an account. The procedure is like opening a bank account, and there are five possible ways to organise your account.

- An individual account in your own name.
- A joint account in your name with someone else such as your spouse.
- A self-managed superannuation fund account if you invest on behalf of a self-managed superannuation fund.
- A trust account if you invest as a trustee of a trust.
- A company account if you invest as a director or secretary on behalf of a company.

You will be asked to provide your Australian residential and postal addresses, an email address, a mobile phone number, your Tax File Number (TFN), and your citizenship status. You will also need 100 points of personal identification, which can usually be done online by referencing your Australian driver's license, Medicare card, passport, or your Australian birth certificate. If you are opening a brokerage account with your bank, they will already have most of the required information. Additional documentation is required for self-managed superannuation accounts, trust accounts, and company accounts.

PLACING AN ORDER

Placing an order with a stockbroker consists of specifying the securities you want to buy or sell, the quantity, and how you want the order handled. If your account is with an online stockbroker, the procedure for placing an order to buy or sell takes place on their website.

- Log into your account and enter your order to buy or sell.
- The order is transmitted to the ASX or in some cases to another market.
- The order is executed at the best possible price.
- Confirmation of the executed order is transmitted directly back to you electronically.

If your account is with a full-service stockbroker, the procedure for placing an order begins by contacting your client advisor by phone or email.

- Instruct your client adviser to enter an order to buy or sell.
- The client adviser enters the order into the stockbroker's computer system and it is transmitted to the ASX or in some cases to another market.
- The order is executed at the best possible price.
- Confirmation of the executed order is transmitted to the client adviser, who in turn reports back to you and confirms it in writing.

The simplest way to buy or to sell securities is with a *market order*. It means the transaction will take place at the best price that is prevailing at the time your order enters the market. If you enter a market order to buy shares, your stockbroker will execute your order for the best *offer* price. If you enter a market order to sell shares, your stockbroker will execute your order for the best *bid* price.

An alternative to a market order is a *limit* order. A limit order to buy establishes the maximum price that you will pay. A limit order to sell establishes the minimum price that you will accept. When you enter a limit order, your stockbroker will get you the best price within the limit that you have set. If they cannot execute the order within your limit, then it will not be filled.

A *stop-loss* order is a conditional order to sell if the price falls to a certain level. You nominate a trigger price and submit an order. If the market price hits your trigger price, a market sell order is executed at the best price. This type of order is used to limit losses and doesn't require the investor to be actively watching the market.

You will also need to specify how long you want an order to remain open. You can lodge an order for the current trading day only, to expire if it is unfilled after a certain date, or to remain good until it is cancelled.

Most investors buy shares they believe are undervalued in anticipation of making a profit from a subsequent increase in price. This is called taking a *long* position. By contrast, an investor who takes a *short* position expects to profit by identifying shares that are overvalued and will subsequently fall in price. A short sale can be a limit order or a market order. Selling short means that you do not own the shares to deliver against the selling contract, so you are obliged to make prior arrangements with your stockbroker before you can place an order for a short sale. When you buy the shares back, you are *covering* your short position.

SETTLEMENT AND TRANSFER

Once an order is executed, the buyer's money needs to be exchanged for the seller's ownership of the shares. This is called *settlement and transfer*. It sounds simple enough, but behind the scenes is a complicated system of clearing transactions. Your stockbroker sends you a buying *contract note* that itemises the cost and the brokerage fees for executing the order. You must pay the amount of the contract note in cleared funds within two business days, so you need to deposit funds with your stockbroker in advance or arrange for the electronic transfer of funds from your bank account. Your stockbroker advises the company's registrar of shareholders that you are now a shareholder. The company includes you on its mailing list for information regularly sent to shareholders such as annual reports, notices of the annual general meeting, and dividends. If you are selling shares, you receive a selling contract note and the proceeds of the sale are deposited into your trading account.

CHESS is the *Clearing House Electronic Sub-register System*. To use CHESS, you need to be sponsored by your stockbroker who will issue you with a *Holder Identification Number* (HIN). You receive a separate holding statement for each company in which you own shares. A statement is issued whenever the amount of the shares you own is altered by a transaction. If you want to have more than one stockbroker, then you will have a different HIN for each one. When you buy a parcel of shares through a particular stockbroker, it is best to resell them through the same stockbroker. If you want to change stockbrokers, however, your CHESS holdings can be transferred to another sponsoring stockbroker.

An alternative to CHESS is *Issuer Sponsored Holding*. It is also an electronic sub-register, but it is sponsored by the issuing company instead of your stockbroker. Each company issues you with a *Security-holder Reference Number* (SRN) that you give to a stockbroker when you trade shares in that company. The company sends you a holding statement for transactions in its shares. If you trade shares in many companies, you will probably find CHESS more convenient than issuer sponsored holdings.

BORROWING TO INVEST

Borrowing to invest is not something that is recommended for first time investors. However, it is a strategy that experienced investors may wish to consider. A *margin loan* enables an investor to borrow money against listed shares and some other securities. They are available from most stockbrokers and the banks. A *Loan to Valuation Ratio* (LVR) applies to each security approved by the lender and determines the maximum amount that can be borrowed against it.

For example, a LVR of 70 percent on a parcel of shares worth $50,000 means that an investor can borrow up to $35,000 if they have $15,000 in cash. If the value of the shares increases by 15 percent, the investor's cash position will increase by 50 percent because it is geared. However, gearing can also magnify losses. If the value of the shares falls so that the amount of borrowing exceeds the LVR, then the investor will receive a *margin call* from the lender. A margin call means they will need to sell some of their shares, lodge additional shares, or deposit enough cash to bring the amount of borrowing back to the LVR.

If you decide to engage in margin lending, compare the features of alternative packages before you sign up. Interest on a margin loan is tax deductible if the borrowed funds are used to buy income-producing securities, and the income can be used to help pay the interest cost. Minimum margin loans are generally between $20,000 and $50,000. Each lender has its own approved list of eligible securities and the LVR for each security on the approved list is rated separately. The maximum LVR is usually 70 percent, but lenders will put a lower LVR on more volatile securities. Most borrowers do not gear up to the maximum LVR because it increases the risk of receiving a margin call.

SUMMARY

Every first time investor has questions about how to buy and sell on the Australian Stockmarket and the purpose of this chapter is to provide some answers. It begins with a description of the four categories of investments including shares, managed investments, options and futures, and fixed income investments.

Choosing a stockbroker usually consists of selecting either an online stockbroker or a full-service stockbroker. A recent alternative has been robo advisors that use computer algorithms to make investment recommendations. Once a stockbroker has been chosen, opening an account is not much different than opening a bank account. Placing an order with a stockbroker consists of specifying the securities you want to buy or sell, the quantity, and how you want the order handled. It can be a market order, a limit order, or a stop-loss order, and it can be for a limited time or good until it is cancelled. After the order is executed, the buyer's funds are exchanged for the seller's ownership in the securities and each receives a contract note from their stockbroker with the details of the transaction.

The chapter concludes with a discussion about borrowing money to invest.

CHAPTER 3

HOW TO FIND
INFORMATION

The practice of investing is driven by information. Unless you
have a professional interest in the financial markets, keeping
fully informed can be a daunting task as the sheer volume
of information is beyond the capacity of most individuals
to absorb. Nor is it always easy to locate the exact piece of
information you need. For a first time investor, the goal is to
be sufficiently informed to be capable of making your own
investment decisions. To find investment information, you need
to know where to look. The purpose of this chapter to show you
where to look.

Private investors have access to information that was
previously only available to large financial institutions. With
the development of the Internet, investment information is
becoming easier to find and cheaper to obtain. Many Internet
sites are designed for private investors, while some offer free
information, and others charge for their services. Here are some
examples of sources of information that are available for private
investors.

- Company reports and websites
- Stockbroker websites
- Newspapers and magazines
- Securities exchange websites
- Analyst research reports
- Free online publications
- Paid online publications
- Google Finance
- Product Disclosure Statements
- Financial advisers
- Online forums and blogs
- MoneySmart website
- Seminars, conferences and expos
- Broadcast media
- Social media
- Yahoo Finance

STOCKBROKER WEBSITES

Stockbroker websites generally offer a range of information such as real-time quotes, company financial data, charting tools, news feeds, and analyst reports. Click on all the tabs to see what kind of information a stockbroker's platform provides and check out any screeners or other tools that will help you find investments that meet your requirements. Some stockbroker websites also offer information in the form of videos, podcasts, user forums, and written articles. If you are an active trader, you may also be able to set up watchlists and receive alert notifications via text or email.

ANALYST REPORTS

Analyst reports can be found on stockbroker websites and subscription services. They either reproduce reports they buy from third-party research firms, or they publish reports that have been compiled by their own analysts. Some research reports concentrate on the analysis of a single company and others cover broader topics such as:

- Economic forecasts
- Equity market themes
- Equity market valuations
- Industry analysis

- Asset allocation recommendations
- Fixed income analysis

Most analysts do not consistently pick winners. One way to increase the odds in your favour is to look for research reports in which several analysts are making similar recommendations. These are called *consensus* recommendations. There is some evidence to suggest that consensus 'buy' recommendations tend to identify stocks that perform above average. You can find consensus recommendations from specialist subscription services such as Market Index at *marketindex.com.au/broker-consensus*.

NEWSPAPERS AND MAGAZINES

The Australian Financial Review is the only comprehensive daily financial newspaper in Australia. The financial section of major newspapers such as *The Age*, *The Sydney Morning Herald* and *The Australian* also offer limited coverage. In addition to print they are also available online. They publish market quotations, general business news, and financial opinion.

The number of investment magazines has dwindled because much of the information they published is now available online. *Money Magazine* at *moneymag.com.au* is Australia's longest-running, best-selling and most-read personal finance magazine. It is available in print and online. *Equity Magazine* at **australianshareholders.com.au/equity** is available in print and online for members of the Australian Shareholders Association. It is highly regarded by retail investors with topical articles written by experts about investing.

Newspapers and magazines are a source of information about broad economic and business trends. News items that reflect overall business conditions include reports about levels of production, retail sales, housing starts or changes in government policy. Other reports may reflect conditions in particular industries such as exploration and production in the mining industry. Important items about individual companies include earnings, dividends, takeovers, new products, management changes, industrial relations, and new financing. Newspapers and magazines not only report information, but they also publish opinion in which they interpret economic developments, analyse trends, examine current developments, and predict future performance.

FREE WEBSITES

The ASX is Australia's largest securities exchange with trading in shares, indices, bonds, hybrids, exchange traded funds, managed funds, warrants, options, and futures. The ASX website at **asx. com.au** is one of the most popular sites in Australia where you can search for information and services including online courses and analysis tools. You can also listen to webcasts and play the sharemarket game. By answering questions about the type of advice you are after and the area in which you live, the Broker

Referral Service will provide you with the names of firms that can help.

There are two other securities exchanges in Australia with their own websites. The Chi-X Exchange website at *chi-x.com.au* offers an alternative to the ASX. The Chi-X investment product platform explains a range of products including Transferable Custody Receipts, shares, warrants, indices, and managed funds. The National Stock Exchange of Australia website at *nsx.com.au* caters for the listing of small to medium enterprises.

The Australian Securities and Investment Commission website at *moneysmart.gov.au* has a comprehensive section for investors. It is a popular website amongst first time investors looking for guidance about the basic principles of investing. The Australian Investors Association has a website at *investors.asn.au* that is designed to provide information that will help its members make better investment decisions.

There are hundreds of free investment blogs and websites, and the mix is constantly changing. An Internet search will reveal websites ranging from genuinely worthwhile to sales gimmickry. Many free websites offer access to an advanced version with more features for a subscription fee.

SUBSCRIPTION WEBSITES

Subscription-based websites offer investment information and advice for a fee. Some have tiered pricing for different levels of service, and they typically offer a free or low-cost trial period to allow you to sample their recommendations. Before you pay for a subscription, look up their track record for recommending worthwhile investments. There are strict rules that apply when it comes to making claims about their investment performance.

Most websites tend to follow a particular investment style. For example, some may promote technology stocks, some may concentrate on resource stocks, and others may focus on approaches to investing such as fundamental or technical analysis. If you come across one that matches your approach to investing, it can be a useful source of information and a way to learn more about investing. Here are a few examples.

- *Morningstar* at **morningstar.com.au**
- *Fat Prophets* at **fatprophets.com.au**
- *The Intelligent Investor* at **intelligentinvestor.com.au**
- *The Motley Fool* Australia at **fool.com.au**
- *Firstlinks* at **firstlinks.com.au**
- *Switzer Report* at **switzerreport.com.au**
- *Incredible Charts* at **incrediblecharts.com**
- *Lincoln Indicators* at **lincolnindicators.com.au**

A *stock screener* is an online tool that sorts through potential investments according to specified criteria to filter out likely candidates. Some are available for free on stockbroker websites and others are on subscription-based websites. Stock screeners can be used to sort qualitative information, financial data, and technical trading indicators. Some deliver alerts when your conditions are met. Stock screeners can save you a lot of time in the search for investment opportunities that match your criteria.

COMPANY INFORMATION

Another source of information is the companies themselves. A *prospectus* is a lengthy legal document that is issued when a company first offers securities for sale to the public. Its purpose is to present the information that investors and their professional advisers require to make an investment decision. In addition to current financial information, a prospectus usually describes the company's future plans.

Most listed companies have a website. However, they vary in the scope and quality of the information provided. Some sites have a strong marketing or product bias. The easiest way to find a company website is by doing an Internet search.

Every public company is required to produce an annual report. In addition to a great deal of window dressing, it contains detailed audited financial statements. The annual report is the most comprehensive form of company information that is readily available to private investors. Several other company reports may also be published including half-year and quarterly interim reports, the chairman's address at the annual general meeting, other announcements and shareholder newsletters. Typically, half-yearly reports come out around February and annual reports around August after the end of the financial year on June 30th. There are a few companies that operate on a different financial year and report at different times, but most of the top 200 companies report at the same time. The information in a company report can have a major impact on its share price, especially if the results are different from expectations or if there is a surprise in management's guidance or outlook statement.

FINANCIAL INDICES

Financial indices provide information about broad changes in the value of securities in different sectors of the stockmarket. A *price index* reflects changes in prices only. An *accumulation index* reflects the reinvestment of interest payments or dividends and measures the total change in accumulated value.

The ASX All Ordinaries Index consists of the largest 500 companies by market capitalisation capturing most of the value of shares traded on the ASX. The All Ordinaries Index is a capitalisation weighted index, which means that larger companies have proportionately more effect than smaller companies. The top ten companies are equivalent to about half of the sample and consequently movements in their share prices have a big effect on movements in the index. The All Ordinaries Index is divided into the Industrials Index and the Resources Index. These are further subdivided into several industry or market sector indexes. The ASX and Standard and Poor have also developed the following *benchmark* indices.

- S&P/ASX 20 consists of the largest 20 companies on the ASX and is used to benchmark targeted investment strategies by institutions and large investors.
- S&P/ASX 50 consists of the largest 50 companies on the ASX and is used to benchmark similar strategies to the ASX20 but with a greater range of shares.
- S&P/ASX 100 is composed of the largest 100 companies and provides a benchmark for portfolios that focus exclusively on large companies with liquid share trading.

- S&P/ASX 200 is made up of the S&P/ASX100 plus another 100 stocks based on liquidity and provides a benchmark for portfolios that include a wider range of shares than the S&P/ASX100. This index is the one most quoted in the financial press.

- S&P/ASX 300 consists of the ASX200 plus another 100 stocks based on liquidity and is used to benchmark portfolios that include smaller capitalised stocks.

- S&P/ASX Small Ordinaries Index consists of the stocks in the ASX300 after removing the stocks in the ASX100. It is used to benchmark portfolios that consist of the shares of smaller companies.

TAXATION

The Australian Tax Office requires investors to keep records of their purchases and sales of securities. It is also in your interest to keep good records to maximise the tax concessions that some securities offer. The effects of taxation on different types of investment earnings is briefly summarised here. However, you should seek professional advice to determine how current tax laws may apply in your circumstances.

Interest payments from bank deposits, debentures, notes, and bonds are included in your assessable income and taxed at your marginal rate. Be sure to quote your Tax File Number if you do not want tax deducted at the top rate.

Dividends from direct shareholdings are taxed at your marginal rate, but you may be entitled to *franking credits* depending on how much tax the company paid. The amount of the dividend and the amount of the franking credit are added together and taxed at your marginal rate before the franking credit is applied to reduce the tax payable. If you are on the top rate of tax, then you will pay some tax on fully franked dividends. If you are on a lower tax rate, you may have surplus franking credits left over that you can use to reduce your tax on other income. You will be advised of the proportion of dividends subject to franking credits when you receive your dividends. Be sure to quote your Tax File Number if you do not want tax deducted at the top rate on the unfranked portion of any dividends.

Capital gains arising from the sale of securities are subject to a capital gains tax. If they are held for less than one year, the total amount of the capital gain is added to your assessable income. If they are held for more than one year, then one-half of the realised capital gain is included in your assessable income. Capital losses can be offset against capital gains in the same or any future tax year, but not against income such as salaries, wages, dividends, or interest.

Income distributions from equity trusts and property trusts are taxed. However, there may also be a flow-on of franking credits or depreciation allowances that make part or all of the distribution tax-free. Tax concessions are available for other investments under prescribed circumstances. These include insurance bonds, friendly society bonds, superannuation funds, rollover funds, allocated pensions and annuities, and pooled development funds. Professional advice is important in assessing the after-tax effectiveness of these investments.

SUMMARY

Information is the driving force behind the stockmarket. The sheer volume and complexity of investment information, however, can be a dilemma for the first time investor. Valuable sources of information include stockbroker websites, financial newspapers and magazines, free websites, subscription websites, and company websites. Financial indices provide information about broad changes in the stockmarket and are used as benchmarks. The chapter concludes with a brief discussion about the taxation implications of investing.

Part B
STARTING OUT IN SHARES

Shares are the starting point for the majority of first time investors. They represent proportional ownership in a company, and they can be transferred from one investor to another without affecting the existence of the company itself. Management control of the company is vested in a board of directors who are elected by the shareholders. As owners, shareholders participate in the company's success through dividends and capital gains. The purpose of Part B is to describe the features of share investments, how to search for value in shares, and how to use technical trading systems.

STARTING OUT IN SHARES

FEATURES OF SHARES

Shares are evidence of ownership in a company. Not all shares are the same because they can differ according to the rights they confer and the obligations they impose on the investor. There are two types of shares – *ordinary shares* and *preference shares.* For each type, there may be more than one class of shares. For example, there may be 'Class A' and 'Class B' ordinary shares.

Some shares are regarded as growth investments whereas others are regarded as income investments. Growth shares generally pay little or no dividends, but they are expected to increase in price, realising a capital gain for the shareholder. Income shares pay large, regular, and reliable dividends. The purpose of this chapter is to describe the features of shares, how they generate income and capital gains, and what kinds of risks are involved.

ORDINARY SHARES

Every public company has ordinary shares, and each ordinary share represents a fractional interest in the company. Ordinary shares confer several rights on the shareholder:

- A shareholder's liability is limited to the amount invested in a fully paid share.
- The right to a proportionate part of the company's profit. It is the Board of Directors who determine if the profits will be distributed in the form of a dividend payment or reinvested in the company.

- The right to a proportionate part of the company's assets, after all the debts are paid, if the company is wound up.

- The right to attend, speak and vote at company shareholder meetings.

- The right to receive prescribed information relating to the company.

- The right to sell the shares, including the right to accept or reject offers under proposed takeovers.

Contributing ordinary shares are only partly paid. For example, a contributing share may be issued at $3.00 with $1.50 payable on subscription and $1.50 payable at *call*. This means that shareholders are legally obliged to pay the remainder of the subscription price when the company asks them to do so. Shareholders in No Liability companies, however, may opt to forfeit their shares instead of paying the call.

Company issued options
Company issued options are not strictly equity securities, rather, they are a means by which an investor can indirectly take a position in a company's shares. Company issued options enable the option holder to take up new shares in the company at a fixed exercise price until an expiry date when the options lapse. Option holders are not yet shareholders because they have not purchased the shares. The advantage is that for a small outlay option holders can benefit from any increase in the share price. The disadvantage is that they have no voting rights or dividend entitlements. Company issued options are occasionally offered as a 'sweetener' during a share float and they trade in the stockmarket along with the company's shares.

Rights issues

Similarly, rights are also not strictly equity securities. Like company issued options, rights issues are a means by which an investor can indirectly take a position in a company's shares. Companies use rights issues to raise additional equity capital from existing shareholders. The rights permit existing shareholders to purchase additional shares at a predetermined price until an expiry date. The new share price is generally at a discount to the current market price and that gives the rights value. A company issues rights to shareholders in proportion to their existing shareholding. In a *renounceable* rights issue, the holder may choose to buy the new shares or sell the rights. In a *non-renounceable* rights issue, the shareholder must either take up the new shares or forfeit the privilege.

PREFERENCE SHARES

Preference shares have a fixed dividend rate. Preference dividends must be paid before dividends on ordinary shares can be paid. Under certain conditions, however, the Board of Directors may decide not to pay the preference dividend. If the company is wound up, preference shareholders rank after debtholders but ahead of ordinary shareholders in the distribution of liquidated assets. Preference shares can take different forms.

- Cumulative preference shares accumulate the liability for dividends that may not have been paid. Ordinary shareholders do not receive ordinary dividends until the arrears in the preference dividends have been paid.
- Non-cumulative preference shares do not accumulate any liability for preference dividends that have not been paid.

- Participating preference shares have the right to receive additional preference dividends depending upon the company's profits.
- Redeemable preference shares may be redeemed by the company under specified conditions.
- Convertible preference shares may be converted into the ordinary shares of the company under specified conditions at the option of the shareholder.
- Converting preference shares automatically convert into the ordinary shares of the company under specified conditions.

INVESTING FOR GROWTH

When a company is doing well, the price of its shares generally reflects its success. A capital gain occurs when an investor sells the shares for a price that is greater than the original cost. Two methods used to identify potential capital gains are *fundamental analysis* and *technical analysis*. Fundamental analysis is concerned with establishing the fair value of a share. Investors using fundamental analysis look for shares that are selling for less than their fair value. Investors using technical analysis look for signals that indicate when to buy or sell.

Fundamental analysis

Fundamental analysis is an attempt to determine a share's fair value. If fair value is greater than a share's current market price, then an investor may decide to buy the shares in anticipation of a capital gain. Fundamental analysis can be approached in two ways – the growth approach or the value approach.

The growth approach says that a company with above-average earnings growth will also experience a higher share price resulting in capital gains. The objective is to identify companies with significant potential for future earnings growth before it becomes reflected in the share price. The growth approach sometimes includes a focus on smaller companies that have few shares outstanding and the potential for rapid earnings growth. Investors who adopt the growth approach are usually looking for shares with an above average price to earnings ratio, below average dividend yield, and above average price to net tangible assets.

The value approach says there are times when a company's share price can be depressed simply because it is out of favour. For example, investors may be avoiding a company's shares because the market appears to favour another company. With fewer buyers and many sellers, the share price becomes low relative to expected earnings and the fair value of the shares is greater than the current market price. Investors who adopt the value approach are usually looking for shares with a below average price to earnings ratio, above average dividend yield, and below average price to net tangible assets.

Technical analysis
Technical analysis is an attempt to determine when a share's price is likely to change. Those who engage in technical analysis include chartists and quantitative analysts who specialise in the investigation of share price cycles and patterns. Technical analysis can be approached in two ways – the market timing approach and the price pattern approach.

The market timing approach says that a company's share price will fluctuate within a normal range. The objective is to buy the shares when the price is near the bottom of its normal range and to sell them near the top of its normal range. In more sophisticated versions, the normal range may be adjusted for other influences such as changes in the business cycle.

The price pattern approach says that share prices tend to produce chart formations that recur. Changes in price patterns are the result of shifts in the balance of supply and demand for the shares. A familiarity with past price patterns can be used to predict future share price movements. Some very sophisticated techniques have been developed to analyse and predict share price patterns.

INVESTING FOR INCOME

When a company is profitable, the ordinary shareholders have a right to share in the profits in proportion to their shareholdings. One way in which ordinary shareholders may share in the profits is the payment of a cash dividend. The Board of Directors decides how much of the profits will be paid out in dividends. Companies generally pay dividends twice each year. The first is a smaller *interim dividend* paid after the middle of the financial year. The second is generally a larger *final dividend* paid after the end of the financial year. In a particularly good year, the Directors may also declare an extra dividend.

When a company declares a dividend, it specifies an amount to be paid per share to shareholders who are listed on the company's share register on the *books closing date*. The shares will be traded and quoted *cum dividend* - with the dividend. One business day before the record date, the shares will be traded and quoted *ex dividend* - without the dividend. When the shares go ex dividend, the buyer is no longer entitled to the dividend, and the share price will generally fall by the amount of the dividend.

The *dividend yield* is the dividend per share for the past year as a percentage of the current share price. Dividend yield is particularly important to income investors and the top yielding shares are regularly reported in the financial press. Keep in mind that some companies pay fully *franked dividends*. This raises the possibility that a low dividend yield which is fully franked may offer a better after-tax return than a higher dividend yield that is not franked. If a company paid dividends of 50 cents per ordinary share over the past twelve months and its current share price is $10.00, then the dividend yield is 5 percent.

$$\text{Dividend yield} = \frac{\text{Current annual dividend}}{\text{Current share price}} = \frac{\$0.50}{\$10.00} = 5 \text{ percent}$$

The proportion of earnings paid out in dividends is the payout ratio. For example, if a company earned $1.00 per share and paid a cash dividend of 50 cents per share, then the payout ratio would be 50 percent. The payout ratio is one way of measuring a firm's dividend policy and comparing it with other firms and industry averages. It reflects the Directors' judgement about how much of the company's profit is paid to shareholders and how much is reinvested in the business.

A company's dividend policy is an important benchmark for investors because it determines the income stream from investing in the shares. Investors also use dividend announcements as information in assessing share value. Sudden changes in dividend policy tend to cause swift changes in share price and the market's reaction to unfavourable dividend announcements is generally greater than for favourable announcements.

Some companies offer a *Dividend Reinvestment Plan* in which you can elect to receive all or part of your dividends in company shares rather than cash. Shares distributed in this way are usually issued at a discount to the ex-dividend share price and the transaction costs are absorbed by the company. The main advantage is that it is an inexpensive and convenient way to accumulate more shares. For the company, it represents the effective sale of new equity and the conservation of cash. Some companies, however, have suspended or eliminated their dividend reinvestment plan because they discovered that increasing the number of shares in this way dilutes earnings per share and may depress the share price.

The main reason that some investors choose preference shares is the relative certainty of dividend income. Preference shareholders rank ahead of ordinary shareholders for a fixed dividend and return of capital. In return for greater certainty, preference shareholders generally give up their claim to participate in the company's growth.

RISK AND RETURN IN SHARES

Most people think of risk as the possibility of losing some or all their money. While that may happen, it is only half of the story because the factors that drive risk are the same factors that drive returns. One way of looking at risk and return is to ask, 'What could cause an investment in these shares to unexpectedly underperform or overperform?' The factors that drive risk and return in shares are economic conditions, industry sector conditions, company performance, and market sentiment.

Economic conditions
Most businesses are cyclical and grow when the economy is expanding and contract when the economy is shrinking. Consumers tend to spend more when they are confident about

CHAPTER 4 - FEATURES OF SHARES

economic growth and job security. Demand for goods and services increases as the economy expands, businesses experience greater sales and earnings, and share prices tend to rise. When economic growth slows down, the reduction in demand translates into lower sales and earnings and share prices tend to fall.

Share prices tend to move in the opposite direction to changes in interest rates. Lower interest rates make borrowing cheaper, encouraging companies to expand, and result in higher share prices. Higher interest rates make borrowing more expensive and tend to depress share prices. Given the low interest rate environment of the past few years, interest rate risk will be a concern if rates rise substantially.

Inflation affects the purchasing power of the returns from shares and consequently affects the price of shares. Modestly rising inflation is generally seen as positive for the broad stockmarket because it is consistent with an economy that is growing at a sustainable pace, but high inflation or unexpected jumps in inflation can result in lower share prices.

The objective is to anticipate the direction and force of the economic tide so that you will be swimming with the current and not fighting against it. An analysis of the economy will not only help you to decide when to enter or exit the stockmarket, but it will also help you predict its impact on individual companies. For the first time investor, a practical approach to understanding the economy is to read the research reports and the financial press with a view to anticipating where economic growth, interest rates and inflation are headed.

Industry sector conditions

A company that operates in a dynamic industry has natural advantages over one in a troubled industry. Changes in the economy do not affect all industry sectors uniformly. For example, rising interest rates are generally bad news for construction, appliance manufacturers or industries that produce capital goods. By contrast, industry sectors like food or health services are not similarly affected. Some industries are directly affected by changes in the economy, others are immune to it, and a few industries are counter-cyclical. Some analysts believe it is more important to be in the right industry sector than in the right stocks.

Attempting to research everything that affects a particular industry sector can be a difficult and time-consuming task. Most of the large stockbrokers and independent advisory services employ security analysts who specialise in particular industry sectors. Their research reports are generally made available to clients and sometimes you will find extracts published in the financial press.

Company performance

When a company is underperforming or the market perception of a company's performance is negative, the share price is likely to fall. The nature of risk varies considerably from one company to another. Rising costs, a product recall, a change in regulations, or falling sales and earnings are examples of adverse changes in a company's circumstances. There is also evidence to suggest that risk is greater for smaller companies and less for larger companies. Although companies in a particular industry sector are subject to many of the same influences, they also reflect differences in corporate personality, competitive profile, and operating results.

The objective is to sift through a promising industry sector in an effort to identify those companies with the best investment potential.

- **Light-weights** are lean, aggressive companies with rapidly increasing sales and profits. They may be riding a wave of industry sector growth, or they may be expanding their market share in a more mature industry. Shares in these companies have volatile prices and pay little or no dividends.

- **Business cyclists** are companies in which sales and earnings expand and contract with the business cycle. Their share price and dividends fluctuate accordingly as they peddle up and down alternating periods of growth and recession.

- **Evergreens** are large, well-established companies that are not significantly affected by the business cycle. They grow at a steady, moderate rate which is reflected in a moderately increasing share price and dividends.

- **Heavy-weights** are also large, established companies but growth has either stopped or reversed. They generate more cash flow than they can profitably reinvest so dividends may indeed be generous. However, the shares do not offer much prospect for capital gains.

- **Walking wounded** are companies that are suffering from an injury to their competitive profile. The cause may be damage from new entrants to the industry, damage from existing competitors, pressure from substitute products and services, price cutting forced by customers' bargaining power, or increased costs forced by suppliers' bargaining power. Their shares are depressed because of the uncertainty about whether they are going to fail or turn around.

If you want to understand the underlying reasons for a company's performance, then you need to know something about them. You can learn much about individual companies by focusing on the following performance drivers.

- **Management** Who is the management team? How much experience to they have? Do they have the skills necessary to make this company perform well? How well have they performed in the past? Do they have a well-articulated plan, or do they simply react to events?

- **Production** Is the company a high-cost or low-cost producer? Is the company a quality producer? Are earnings substantially influenced by the cost or availability of raw materials? Are wages a significant component of production? Does the company face aggressive trade unions? Does the company benefit from technology in the production process? Is there enough capacity to achieve the growth targets?

- **Marketing** Is the main market industrial, commercial or consumer? Does the company depend on a few large customers or many small ones? Is the product line diversified or specialised? Do the company's products have a good reputation and customer brand loyalty? Is the market large enough to sustain sales growth? How aggressive is the marketing effort and what is the rate of sales growth?

- **Investment** How is the company improving its product line and productive capacity? How much is spent on research and development? What new products or new applications of existing products are in the pipeline? How much is spent on new plant and equipment and how will modernisation and expansion improve the company's earning power.

54

- **Government regulation** How much does government policy affect earnings? Are sales affected by domestic incentives such as subsidies, or overseas restrictions such as tariffs? To what extent do government agencies dictate how the company may operate and what prices it may charge? How do the government's monetary and fiscal policies affect the company?

Market sentiment

Market sentiment is a cyclical effect in the stockmarket that is essentially driven by human emotion. Swings in market sentiment have characteristically been explained by fear and greed. They reflect sweeping changes in investor expectations and the chance that the entire stockmarket will surge or crash as a result. When market sentiment is optimistic it is characterised as a 'bull market', and when it is pessimistic it is characterised as a 'bear market'. Swings in market sentiment in either extreme causes share prices to deviate from their fair value.

Changes in market sentiment usually occur unexpectedly and the impact is widespread. For example, the Australian stockmarket crashed by nearly one-third when market sentiment plunged at the beginning of the Pandemic. However, a reversal in market sentiment quickly resulted in surging share prices. The market recovered its lost ground in just over a year, and rose 50 percent above its Pandemic low. This is an example of the entire stockmarket unexpectedly crashing and surging because of changes in market sentiment.

Given that market sentiment is a collective intangible human emotion, it does not lend itself to objective measurement or prediction. However, there are a few technical indicators that are used to gather information about which direction prices are moving and when they are reaching extremes. These are discussed in Chapter 6 on technical analysis including the advance-decline line, the high/low index, trading volume, moving averages and various oscillators. A different type of measure is the VIX, or Fear Index, that uses options data to measure market sentiment.

Beta factor as a measure of risk and return

A high degree of uncertainty about future returns causes investors to change their minds more frequently resulting in increased trading and greater price volatility. The *beta factor* measures the relative volatility of returns for an individual share compared with the volatility of returns for the overall market. Shares with a beta that is greater than 1.0 are more volatile than the market average. They would be expected to gain value faster in a rising market and they would be expected to lose value faster in a falling market. Shares with a beta that is less than 1.0 are less volatile than the market average. They would be expected to gain value more slowly in a rising market and they would be expected to lose value more slowly in a falling market.

Your stockbroker may have beta factors for individual shares and there are subscription websites that provide regularly updated betas. The calculation of beta is not only complex, but it is also plagued by several methodological difficulties that weaken its reliability. University academics have enthusiastically studied betas for a long time, however most investors have yet to fully embrace this measure of investment risk.

Risk-return trade-off

The risk-return trade-off means finding the balance between minimising risk and maximising returns. Lower levels of risk are usually associated with lower returns and higher levels of risk are usually associated with higher returns. However, taking on higher levels of risk does not automatically lead to higher returns. The risk-return trade-off only implies that high risk shares have the possibility of realising higher returns. There is no guarantee that it will happen.

The most basic and effective strategy for minimising risk is *diversification*. It is based on the proposition that a well-diversified portfolio consists of different investments in which the returns are not correlated. That means they do not all move in the same direction at the same time. Instead, they tend to offset each other so that the overall risk of the portfolio is minimised. Combining cyclical and countercyclical investments reduces economic risks, combining different industry sectors reduces industry risks, and combining different kinds of companies reduces company risk. While diversification is an important component in minimising risk, it does not guarantee that there will never be a loss.

SUMMARY

Shares are evidence of ownership in a company. They consist of ordinary shares and preference shares. Some shares are regarded as growth investments because they are expected to increase in price realising a capital gain for the shareholder. Two methods that are used to identify potential capital gains are *fundamental analysis* and *technical analysis*. Some shares are regarded as income investments because they pay large, regular, and reliable dividends. A company's dividend policy is an important benchmark for income investors because it determines the income stream from investing in the company's shares. The tradeoff between risk and return in shares means finding the balance between minimising risk and maximising returns. The factors that drive risk and return are economic conditions, industry sector conditions, company performance, and market sentiment. An effective strategy for minimising risk is diversification. Lower levels of risk are generally associated with lower returns and higher levels of risk are generally associated with higher returns.

CHAPTER 5

FUNDAMENTAL ANALYSIS

The main purpose of fundamental analysis is to estimate the fair value of a company's shares. When an estimate of fair value is established, it can be compared to the current market price to decide if the shares are a candidate for investment. An important part of fundamental analysis is the evaluation of financial statements. A widely practiced method of analysing and interpreting financial statements is by using ratios to assess operating performance, liquidity and solvency, and value indicators. An example is presented comparing fair value to market price using the earnings approach and the present value approach. The chapter concludes with a description of special situations that suggest there is a potential for capital gain.

FINANCIAL STATEMENTS

It may come as a shock to discover that most of the advisers who make investment recommendations have never actually read the company's financial statements. They generally depend on security analysts for this information. As a first time investor, you may want to take a similar approach. At the very least, you need to know enough to understand the comments made by analysts.

Audited company financial statements are a statement of opinion, not a statement of fact. Their intent is to present a true and fair picture of the company. However, the application of generally accepted accounting principles is neither consistent nor free from manipulation. For these reasons, great care and judgement is needed in the evaluation of company financial statements.

Income statement

An income statement is a company's most important financial statement because it discloses how much the company has earned or lost for its shareholders over a specific period. Figure 5.1 is an income statement for Typical Company Ltd.

The income statement discloses the operating revenue and the operating expenses that result in an operating profit or loss before tax for the year. There may also be an *abnormal* profit or loss reported that is part of the company's operations but is abnormal by reason of its size and effect on the operating profit. The operating profit is subject to tax, leaving the operating profit (or loss) after income tax. There may also be some *extraordinary* items net of income tax reported. These are very rare items of revenue and expense that are outside the ordinary operations of the company and not of a recurring nature.

Figure 5.1 Income statement

TYPICAL COMPANY LTD
INCOME STATEMENT
For the Year Ending 30 June 202X

		$ million
Operating revenue		**480**
Operating expenses		
Cost of sale	315	
Interest	5	
Depreciation	10	
Other	<u>80</u>	**<u>(410)</u>**
Operating profit before abnormal items and income tax		70
Abnormal profit (loss) before income tax		<u>(30)</u>
Operating profit before income tax		**40**
Income tax attributable to operating profit		<u>(16)</u>
Operating profit after income tax		**24**
Extraordinary profit (loss) after tax		<u>(17)</u>
Operating profit and extraordinary items after income tax		**7**
Retained profits at the beginning of the financial year		<u>61</u>
Total available for appropriation		**68**
Dividends provided for or paid		<u>(12)</u>
Retained profits at the end of the financial year		**56**

The operating profit and extraordinary items after income tax represents the profit for the period attributable to the ordinary shareholder. To this amount is added retained profits (or accumulated losses) at the beginning of the financial year and any amounts transferred from reserves resulting in the total available for appropriation. The total available for appropriation may be used for dividends, transfers to reserves and other appropriations or kept in the company as retained profits (or accumulated losses) at the end of the financial year. This last amount also appears in the shareholders' equity section of the balance sheet.

Despite the importance of the income statement, it cannot always be relied upon as an accurate measurement of a company's earnings. Financial analysts refer to 'quality of earnings' when they assess the reliability of a company's income statement. They favour financial statements of companies with the following characteristics.

- Consistent, conservative, and prudent accounting policies.
- Earnings that are stable, predictable, and derived from the firm's core operations.
- Sales that convert quickly into cash.
- Earnings that are not driven by tax factors or gains from currency or price movements.
- A capital structure that has not been manipulated to create earnings.

Security analysts may question the quality of reported earnings for companies with one or more of the following warning signals.

- An audit report that is too long, unusually worded or delayed.
- The appointment of a new auditor.
- Changes to less conservative accounting policies.
- Unusual increases in liability accounts or intangible assets.
- Non-recurring income such as asset sales.
- Significant decline in things like research and development, advertising, gross margin, liquid assets, or asset turnover.
- Significant movements in reserves.

Balance sheet

A balance sheet discloses what a company owns and how it has been financed by its creditors and shareholders. Figure 5.2 is a balance sheet for Typical Company Ltd. It begins with the assets, or what the company owns, consisting of current assets and non-current assets. From this is subtracted the liabilities, or what the company owes, consisting of current liabilities and non-current liabilities. The difference between assets and liabilities is equal to shareholders' equity consisting of share capital, reserves, and retained profits or accumulated losses.

Figure 5.2 Balance sheet

TYPICAL COMPANY LTD
BALANCE SHEET
As at 30 June 202X

		$ million
ASSETS		
Current		
Cash	6	
Receivables	24	
Inventories	<u>30</u>	60
Non-Current		
Investments	30	
Property, plant and equipment	50	
Intangibles	<u>20</u>	100
Total assets		**<u>160</u>**
LIABILITIES		
Current		
Creditors and borrowings	10	
Provision for income tax	8	
Provision for dividend	<u>12</u>	30
Non-Current		
Creditors and borrowings		<u>34</u>
Total liabilities		**64**
SHAREHOLDERS EQUITY		
Ordinary shares	40	
Retained profits	<u>56</u>	<u>96</u>
Total liabilities and shareholder's equity		**<u>160</u>**

The main function of the balance sheet is to disclose how much the company is worth using generally accepted accounting principles. One of these principles is depreciated or amortised historical cost as the basis for valuing some of the non-current assets. This generally results in a book value for the company that is vastly different from its market value. Unless a company expends funds on the purchase or development of an asset, it may not even be shown on the balance sheet. Similarly, increases in asset value because of inflation may not be shown. Sometimes these hidden assets represent a significant contribution to a company's worth.

Statement of cash flow
A statement of cash flow complements the balance sheet and the income statement. It is a reconciliation of the closing cash balance in the balance sheet, and it can be used to assess the ability of the company to generate cash flow. It is more reliable than the income statement because it is subject to less interpretation of generally accepted accounting principles. Figure 5.3 is a statement of cash flow for Typical Company Ltd. Cash flow from operating activities is generally the main source of cash flow. It consists of receipts from customers, payments to suppliers, salaries and wages, interest payments and taxes. It also includes any changes in net working capital. Cash flow from investing activities includes the purchase and/or sale of non-current assets. It is not unusual for a company to have negative cash flow from investing activities related to the acquisition of long-term assets. Cash flow from financing activities includes borrowing and repayment, share issues and buybacks, and dividends.

Figure 5.3 Statement of cash flow

TYPICAL COMPANY LTD
STATEMENT OF CASH FLOW
For the Year Ending 30 June 202X

		$ million
Cash flow from operating activities		
Receipts from customers	480	
Payments to suppliers	(300)	
Salaries and wages paid	(150)	
Interest Paid	(5)	
Taxes Paid	(15)	10
Cash flow from investing activities		
Payments for property, plant and equipment		(50)
Cash flow from financing activities		
Proceeds from borrowing	34	
Dividends paid	(12)	22
Net increase (decrease) in cash		(18)
Cash at the beginning of the year		24
Cash at the end of the year		6

The statement of cash flow is a good check on the income statement. It is possible for the income statement to show a profit when cash flow is negative. If the cash flowing into a company exceeds the cash flowing out, then it can continue to operate regardless of its profitability. However, if the cash flowing out of a company repeatedly exceeds the cash flowing in, then eventually the company will run out of cash and grind to a halt. Profits are not cash, and that is why the statement of cash flow is a valuable check on the other financial reports.

OPERATING PERFORMANCE

The most widely practiced method of analysing and interpreting financial statements is by using ratios. What we need to make judgements about good or bad financial ratios is something with which to compare them. Comparisons with past financial ratios tell us if the trends are getting better or worse. Comparisons with the financial ratios of similar firms or industry averages tell us how well a company stacks up against the performance of other companies in the same line of business. Comparisons with rule-of-thumb standards tell us how a company equates with commonly accepted benchmarks. An analysis of operating performance focuses upon profitability, efficiency, and the effects of financial leverage. It consists of finding answers to several questions.

- How profitable is each dollar of sales?
- How efficiently do the assets generate sales?
- How do profitability and efficiency combine to produce a return on the investment in assets?
- What proportion of the assets have been funded by the shareholders?
- How much does borrowing leverage the return on assets into a return for the shareholders?

Operating profit margin

This ratio represents the average operating profit per dollar of operating revenue. Extraordinary items are not included because they would distort the analysis of operating performance. Typical Company's operating profit margin is 5 percent.

$$\text{Operating profit margin} = \frac{\text{Operating profit after tax}}{\text{Operating revenue}} = \frac{\$24,000,000}{\$480,000,000} = 5 \text{ percent}$$

Operating profit margin can vary significantly from one type of business to another. Look for an operating profit margin that not only compares favourably with other firms in the same industry sector but also improves over time.

Asset turnover

Asset turnover measures how hard the company's asset base is working to generate sales. Typical Company's asset turnover is 3 times.

$$\text{Asset turnover} = \frac{\text{Operating revenue}}{\text{Total assets}} = \frac{\$480,000,000}{\$160,000,000} = 3 \text{ times}$$

Greater asset turnover indicates more efficient use of assets to generate sales, and less asset turnover indicates less efficient use of assets to generate sales. The rate of asset turnover varies significantly from one industry sector to another, so we are looking for companies that compare favourably with other companies in the same industry sector and improve over time.

Return on assets

This ratio is used to assess the profit earning performance of the company's assets. It relates the operating profit after tax to the investment in assets. We are looking for a return on assets that not only compares favourably with other firms in the same industry sector, but also improves over time. Typical Company's return on assets is 15 percent.

$$\text{Return on assets} = \frac{\text{Operating profit after tax}}{\text{Total assets}} = \frac{\$24,000,000}{\$160,000,000} = 15 \text{ percent}$$

Return on assets can also be found by multiplying the operating profit margin by the asset turnover.

$$\text{Return on assets} = \text{Operating profit margin} \times \text{Asset turnover}$$
$$= 5 \text{ percent} \times 3 \text{ times} = 15 \text{ percent}$$

Return on assets links the dynamic relationship between operating revenue, costs, and profits with the underlying asset base. A decline in the return on assets will occur if sales fall or expenses rise faster than sales. A decline can also occur if the investment in assets increases at a faster rate than operating profit after tax.

Shareholders' interest

Most companies make use of borrowed capital. Borrowing not only makes it possible to leverage the shareholder's equity, but also enables the company to finance opportunities that would otherwise have to be forgone. The proportions of debt and equity capital in financing the company's assets is usually referred to as its *financial structure*. One way of looking at financial structure is to focus on the proportion of total assets represented by the shareholder's interest. For Typical Company Ltd it is 60 percent.

$$\text{Shareholders' interest} = \frac{\text{Shareholders' equity}}{\text{Total assets}} = \frac{\$96,000,000}{\$160,000,000} = 60 \text{ percent}$$

If shareholders have financed 60 percent of the company's assets, then creditors have financed the remaining 40 percent. An important and difficult question for both management and investors is how much debt is too much debt. The acceptable proportion of debt varies between different industry sectors. Debt finance can enable a company to grow and to improve its profitability, but too much debt exposes it to the risk of financial loss and potential insolvency.

Return on shareholder's equity

This ratio is one of the best indicators of overall performance. It reflects the earning power of the shareholders' investment in the company and can be compared with the return from any alternative investment. If there are no liabilities, the return on shareholder's equity would be the same as the return on assets. However, return on shareholder's equity is amplified by the extent to which the company has borrowed or leveraged its equity. Typical Company's return on shareholders' equity is 25 percent.

$$\text{Return on shareholders' equity} = \frac{\text{Operating profit after tax}}{\text{Shareholders equity}} = \frac{\$24,000,000}{\$96,000,000} = 25 \text{ percent}$$

Return on shareholders' equity can also be found by dividing return on assets by shareholders' interest. These underlying ratios can be used to explain any changes in the return on shareholders' equity.

$$\text{Return on shareholders' equity} = \frac{\text{Return on assets}}{\text{Shareholders' interest}} = \frac{15 \text{ percent}}{60 \text{ percent}} = 25 \text{ percent}$$

Operating performance model

The operating performance model represents a framework for organising the analysis of these ratios. It is a powerful tool that can be used to identify important variables in a company's financial statements, determine the cause and effect between those variables and direct your attention toward changes that may affect the value of the company's securities. Figure 5.4 is the operating performance model for Typical Company Ltd.

The objective is to maximise return on shareholders' equity. It is composed of two drivers - return on assets and shareholders' interest. Return on assets is an overall measure of

70

how well the company's asset base produces a profit. It reflects operating decisions over buying, selling, expense control and asset management. Shareholders' interest is a measure of the shareholders' investment in the company's asset base. It reflects financing decisions over how much capital has been borrowed and the degree to which the company has leveraged its financial structure.

Figure 5.4 Operating performance model

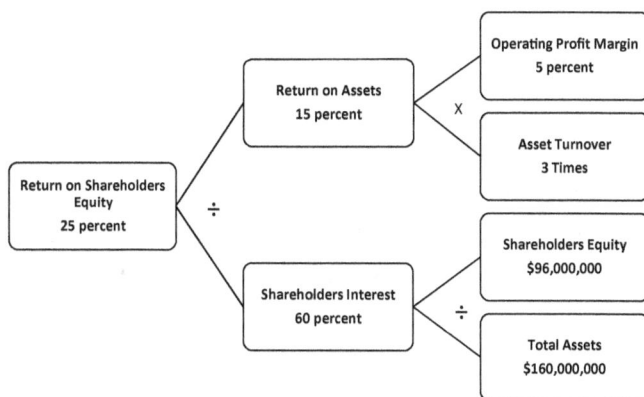

LIQUIDITY AND SOLVENCY

Liquidity ratios reflect the ability of a company to meet its current financial commitments whereas solvency ratios take a longer view and are particularly important to holders of the company's fixed income securities. Inability to satisfy the legitimate demands of creditors is sufficient reason for a company to be wound up. These ratios, therefore, are mostly concerned with the financial health of the company and its 'survivalability'. They should be evaluated in conjunction with the statement of cash flow.

Current ratio

The current ratio is a commonly used test of liquidity since it indicates the extent to which the claims of short-term creditors are covered by assets that can be quickly converted into cash. Typical company's current ratio is 2 to 1.

$$\text{Current ratio} = \frac{\text{Current assets}}{\text{Current liabilities}} = \frac{\$60,000,000}{\$30,000,000} = 2 \text{ to } 1$$

A current ratio of 2 to 1 means that current assets equal twice the current liabilities, and the generally accepted rule of thumb is that the current ratio should be about 2 to 1 or better. If a company has growing sales and a short cash cycle, however, then a lower current ratio can be satisfactory.

Liquid ratio or acid test

Creditors often question the liquidity of a company's inventory. They reason that since inventory is two steps away from cash it should not be considered available to pay bills that are immediately due. They prefer to use the liquid ratio or acid test in which inventory is subtracted from the current assets. Typical Company's liquid ratio is 1 to 1.

$$\text{Liquid ratio} = \frac{\text{Current assets} - \text{Inventory}}{\text{Current liabilities}} = \frac{\$60,000,000 - \$30,000,000}{\$30,000,000} = 1 \text{ to } 1$$

The rule of thumb for the liquid ratio is 1 to 1. While it needs to be interpreted with the same care as the current ratio, significant deviations below 1 are usually viewed with concern.

Net working capital to sales

A company needs to maintain enough working capital to adequately service its sales volume. If net working capital declines relative to sales, there may be an impending liquidity problem. Net working capital is the difference between current assets and current liabilities. Typical Company's net working capital to sales is 6.25 cents per dollar of sales.

$$\text{Net working capital to sales} = \frac{\text{Current assets} - \text{Current liabilities}}{\text{Operating revenue}}$$

$$\frac{\$60,000,000 - \$30,000,000}{\$460,000,000} = 6.25 \text{ cents}$$

In this example, net working capital to sales may be a bit low at 6.25 cents per dollar of sales. Although the current ratio and quick ratio are normal, the net working capital to sales ratio would tell us to keep an eye on the company's liquidity. If the ratio is trending downward, our concern would be even greater.

Interest cover

The interest cover ratio measures the extent to which earnings are available to pay the fixed interest charges. Failure to meet this obligation usually results in legal action by creditors. The ratio is found by dividing earnings before interest and taxes (EBIT) by the amount of the fixed interest charges. EBIT is found by adding the interest charges back to operating profit before income tax. The interest cover ratio for Typical Company is comfortable because there are enough earnings before interest and taxes to pay the fixed interest nine times over.

$$\text{Interest cover} = \frac{\text{EBIT}}{\text{Interest}} = \frac{\$45,000,000}{\$5,000,000} = 9 \text{ times}$$

Debt to equity ratio

The debt to equity ratio is another way of looking at capital structure. It is used to measure the amount of long-term borrowing compared with shareholders' equity. The lower the debt to equity ratio, the less likelihood of insolvency. Debt to equity ratios vary substantially and should be compared with the average for the industry sector. The debt to equity ratio for Typical Company Ltd is 35.4 percent.

$$\text{Debt to equity ratio} = \frac{\text{Non Current liabilities}}{\text{Shareholders equity}} = \frac{\$34,000,000}{\$96,000,000} = 35.4 \text{ percent}$$

VALUE INDICATORS

Value indicators relate the information in the company's financial statements to the company's ordinary shares. Let us assume that the price of Typical Company Ltd shares is $8.00. An important part of fundamental analysis is to evaluate the market value of the shares in terms of the information disclosed in the company financial reports.

Dividend payout

The dividend payout is the proportion of annual operating profit after tax that is paid out in dividends to the ordinary shareholders. It reflects the dividend policy of the company that results in income to shareholders. Typical company's payout is 50 percent

$$\text{Dividend payout} = \frac{\text{Dividends provided for or paid}}{\text{Operating profit after tax}} = \frac{\$12,000,000}{\$24,000,000} = 50 \text{ percent}$$

Dividends per share (DPS)

This is the amount of dividends provided for or paid in the past year divided by the average number of ordinary shares outstanding. The dividend for Typical Company is 40 cents per share.

$$\text{Dividend per share} = \frac{\text{Dividends provided for or paid}}{\text{Ordinary shares outstanding}} = \frac{\$12,000,000}{30,000,000} = 40 \text{ cents}$$

Dividend yield

The dividend yield reflects the income producing capacity of a share based on the annual dividend and the current share price. The dividend yield for Typical Company Ltd shares is 5 percent.

$$\text{Dividend yield} = \frac{\text{Dividend per share}}{\text{Share price}} = \frac{\$0.40}{\$8.00} = 5 \text{ percent}$$

Earnings per share (EPS)

Investors are more interested in earnings per share than in total earnings. Earnings per share can be found by dividing annual operating profit after tax by the number of ordinary shares outstanding. Earnings per share is not only affected by changes in profitability, but also by changes in the number of shares outstanding. Earnings per share for Typical Company Ltd shares is 80 cents.

$$\text{Earnings per share} = \frac{\text{Operating profit after tax}}{\text{Ordinary shares outstanding}} = \frac{\$24,000,000}{30,000,000} = 80 \text{ cents}$$

Earnings per share growth rate

The earnings per share growth rate measures how much per share earnings can grow without further outside financing. It can be estimated by multiplying the return on shareholders' equity by the retention rate. The retention rate is equal to 100 percent minus the dividend payout. The EPS growth rate for Typical Company Ltd is 12.5 percent.

$$\text{Earnings per share growth rate} = \text{Return on shareholders' equity x Retention rate}$$
$$= 25\% \times (100\% - 50\%) = 12.5 \text{ percent}$$

An estimate of the current earnings growth rate is important, but what really matters is any change that might be expected. If the growth rate is expected to be different in the future, then the expected growth rate should be used. The Operating Performance Model provides an excellent framework for anticipating changes in return on shareholders' equity which is the key to future changes in the EPS growth rate.

Price to earnings ratio (P/E ratio)

The P/E ratio expresses the current share price as a multiple of the most recent annual earnings per share. The P/E ratio for Typical Company Ltd shares is 10 times.

$$\text{Price to earnings ratio} = \frac{\text{Share price}}{\text{Earnings per share}} = \frac{\$8.00}{\$0.80} = 10 \text{ times}$$

The P/E ratio is often used as a means of measuring investors' expectations of future performance. A low P/E ratio is an indication that investors are not optimistic about future performance. A high P/E ratio generally indicates positive investor optimism about future performance.

Price earnings growth ratio (PEG ratio)

The price earnings growth ratio is the relationship of the P/E ratio to the earnings per share growth rate as a whole number. For Typical Company Ltd it is 0.8.

$$\text{PEG Ratio} = \frac{\text{P/E ratio}}{\text{EPS growth rate}} = \frac{10}{12.5} = 0.8$$

In general, the P/E ratio should be equal to the long term earnings per share growth rate, so a ratio of 1.0 represents fair value. A PEG ratio less than 1.0 means that the share is under-priced relative to fair value, and a PEG more than 1.0 means that the share is overpriced relative to fair value.

Net asset backing per share (NAB)
Net asset backing per share tells us what an ordinary share would be worth if all the assets were sold at their balance sheet values and the debts were repaid. Intangible assets are excluded on the conservative premise that they may have no realisable value. Net asset value for Typical Company Ltd is $2.53 per share.

$$\text{Net asset backing} = \frac{\text{Assets} - \text{Liabilities} - \text{Intangibles}}{\text{Ordinary shares outstanding}}$$

$$\frac{\$160,000,000 - \$64,000,000 - \$20,000,000}{30,000,000} = \$2.53$$

The price to net asset backing reflects the relationship between the share price and the net assets per share. A company with strong management that functions efficiently and profitably should have a price to net asset backing that is greater than 1. The price to net asset backing for Typical Company Ltd is 3.16 times.

$$\text{Price to net asset backing} = \frac{\text{Current share price}}{\text{Net assets per share}} = \frac{\$8.00}{\$2.53} = 3.16 \text{ times}$$

VALUE VERSUS PRICE

Price and value are not the same thing. If the fair value of a share is significantly greater than its market price, an investor may decide to buy them in anticipation of a capital gain. If fair value is less than market price, they may avoid the shares or sell any shares that they own.

For years, the academic community has been trying to convince itself and investors that the stockmarket prices shares 'efficiently'. The implication being that a share's price is a true reflection of its fair value and that it is fruitless to look for shares that are mispriced. However, share prices do diverge from their fair value and there are plenty of historical examples to illustrate the point. In practice, establishing the fair value of a share is more of an art than a precise science. It has a great deal more to do with making judgements about things that may happen in the future than it does with merely analysing current facts. The ability to foresee likely future events and their effect on a company's share price is the key element in successfully searching for value.

There are several established methods for estimating the fair value of a share. We shall focus on two approaches that are appropriate for the shares of publicly listed companies. They are the earnings approach and the present value approach. Both need to be applied with caution, however, because they are very sensitive to variations in the input variables.

Earnings approach

The earnings approach is suitable for valuing shares in companies with stable earnings per share (EPS) and requires two input variables. The first is an estimate of the most likely EPS that the company can be expected to achieve during the holding period. The second is an estimate of the most likely P/E ratio that the market will place on the company's shares.

Typical Company Ltd has an EPS of 80 cents. The historical EPS growth rate has been 12.5 percent per year. Therefore, if things continue as before, then the expected EPS for next year will be $0.80 x 1.125 = 90 cents. Typical Company Ltd has a current market price of $8.00 per share and a current P/E ratio of 10 times. The most important influences on the future P/E ratio are the firm's dividend policy, the rate of growth in earnings per share and the degree of certainty about expected future earnings. Fair value using the earnings approach consists of multiplying the expected EPS by the expected P/E ratio. The estimate of fair value for Typical Company shares is $9.00. It exceeds the market price of $8.00 by $1.00.

Fair value = Expected EPS x Expected P/E ratio = $0.90 x 10 = $9.00

Present value approach

Fair value based on the present value approach is valuable as a cross-check on the earnings approach. It consists of finding the present value of expected future dividends and the expected future resale price of the shares. The present value approach discounts the future cash flows according to a required rate of return based on a risk-free rate of return plus a risk premium. The risk-free rate of return is usually regarded as the yield on a Commonwealth Treasury Note. In our example, the risk-free rate of return is estimated to be 4 percent and the risk premium is estimated to be 12 percent resulting in a 16 percent required rate of return.

The example in Figure 5.5 illustrates a forecast for the expected dividends and share price over a three-year holding period. Typical Company Ltd is expected to lift its EPS growth rate from 12.5 percent to 15 percent for each of the next three years. The payout ratio is expected to remain at 50 percent of EPS resulting in the forecast for dividends. If the expected P/E ratio remains at 10 times, then the forecast share price at the end of Year 3 will be $12.20.

Figure 5.5 Forecasting expected results

	Current Year actual	Year 1 forecast	Year 2 forecast	Year 3 forecast
EPS growth rate	12.5%	15%	15%	15%
EPS	$0.80	$0.92	$1.06	$1.22
Payout	50%	50%	50%	50%
Dividends	$0.40	**$0.46**	**$0.53**	**$0.61**
P/E ratio	10 times			10 times
Share Price	$8.00			**$12.20**

The required rate of return is used as a discount rate to find the present value of the expected dividends and the expected resale price. The estimate of fair value is $9.00, which exceeds the current market price of $8.00 by $1.00.

$$\text{Fair value} = \frac{\$0.46}{1.16} + \frac{\$0.53}{(1.16)^2} + \frac{\$0.61 + \$12.20}{(1.16)^3} = \$9.00$$

In these examples, the earning approach and the present value approach have produced the same result. It is unlikely that this would occur in practice. Both are sensitive to different input variables which are themselves estimates of future values.

SPECIAL SITUATIONS

Special situations are circumstances that suggest there is potential for a capital gain. The competition to discover them is intense and there are lots of big game hunters out there looking for the same quarry. The trick is to get in before the conditions that create these opportunities are generally appreciated. Here are some examples.

Cash cows

These are shares with a market price that is below the company's net working capital per share. These companies are loaded with cash, and they are particularly attractive because they have the opportunity to make profitable acquisitions or investments. They are also candidates for a merger or takeover offer by others who have good investment opportunities but not the cash to fulfil them. If they also have a large tax loss carry forward credit, then they are an outstanding candidate.

Thin capitalisation

These are companies with relatively few shares outstanding. Trading in their shares is thin and the share price is generally volatile. Therefore, any positive development is likely to be reflected by a substantial increase in the share price. These shares are also good candidates for a share split if the current price is relatively high.

New floats

Many *initial public offerings* (IPOs) are floated each year. The strong likelihood that a share issue will move toward listing is a positive step because it will need to fulfil the listing requirements implying a certain amount of corporate strength. It will also trade in a market with wider exposure and come under the gaze of more investors. There is evidence that most new floats are under priced. This all helps to create demand for the shares resulting in a higher price.

Small company growth

Significant growth potential is usually associated with companies that are young, small, and not well-known. Although many large, established companies also possess attractive growth potential, their share price tends to reflect this condition.

Under-valued assets

Companies carry assets on their books at the price for which they were originally purchased. This is called *book value*. If the asset has increased in value since it was purchased, then its market value may be substantially greater than its book value. If the asset is sold, the company will realise a capital gain on the sale that translates into the share price. Sometimes the market and even the company itself may fail to comprehend the value of an asset. Under-valued assets occur most often among oil, mining, and other resource shares.

Changes in management or policy

A poor company with good management is more likely to represent an investment opportunity than a good company with poor management. Changes in management can sometimes produce a signal that new developments are about to occur. The intention of a company to diversify its activities into a promising line of business would represent a potentially favourable policy change.

Hidden earnings

Occasionally the market fails to recognise a turnaround in a company's earnings. Of course, this only persists until the next earnings report is issued. For example, when the price of a commodity rises sharply those companies producing that commodity experience a substantial increase in earnings. There is a time lag between the increase in the commodity price and a reported increase in the company's earnings.

Buybacks

A buyback consists of a company offering to purchase some of its own ordinary shares. The effect of a buyback is to reduce the number of shares outstanding thereby increasing the earnings per share for the remaining shares. This should lead to a higher share price. Buybacks are generally the result of a company that has a large cash balance and no developments in which to invest. Some companies buy the shares in small parcels over time, others offer shareholders a premium to the market price.

Technology
Any radical change in technology implies a possibility for investment opportunities. New products or processes and the impact of high-technology developments in medicine, aerospace, oceanography, and computers are good examples.

Legal and political events
Profitable opportunities may arise when a change in the tax law benefits a particular industry or company. Similarly, changes in tariffs and other forms of protection from foreign competition may also create the same effect. Shareholders may profit if a court case is resolved in favour of their company. Anything that would markedly boost earnings or increase assets (like a ruling involving a patent, a valuable mining lease or a reduction in tax liabilities) is in this category.

Takeovers
Most corporate weddings are friendly, with a courtship and a mutual agreement on the merger contract. This permits both companies to calmly work out terms intended to benefit everyone. Sometimes one company decides to acquire another company without bothering to negotiate. A takeover can occur as an off-market offer directly to all shareholders, or it can be an on-market offer to buy shares on the exchange.

A sudden offer for another company's shares with no advanced notice is an aggressive act. Investors may view the bidder favourably but the management of the firm under siege is likely to cry 'raid'. Then the air will be filled with the thunder of charges and counter-charges. If the management of the company that is on the defensive thinks that it may lose control, it may quickly find a merger partner that is more to its liking. The offer price, in cash or securities, is usually well above the current market price because shareholders are unlikely to accept the offer unless they will benefit, and the acquiring company will not make an offer unless it sees good value.

Rumours often precede the announcement of merger negotiations but there is rarely much warning of a surprise takeover bid. Occasionally there is a leak, or a few outsiders are shrewd enough to detect that something is going on causing an otherwise unexplained rise in the share price. After the announcement, the target company shares will rise to reflect the terms of the offer. If there is any doubt about the deal going through, however, the price will not rise all the way. In a takeover bid for cash, the shares will automatically rise to the bid price if the cash payment is immediately available.

Share splits and bonus issues

Share splits and bonus issues represent additional shares issued by a company to its shareholders for no extra cost. No value is created because the market price automatically adjusts for the increased number of shares outstanding. It is like trading a $10 note for two $5 notes. However, there are more subtle benefits. First, some shareholders believe that they have received additional shares for free and regard this as a signal that the company is doing well. Second, if a company cannot afford to pay a cash dividend, it may use a split or a bonus share issue to appease shareholders for the loss of the expected cash dividend. Third, if the dividend per share is maintained after a split or a bonus share issue, then shareholders have effectively received an increase in the dividend.

SUMMARY

The search for value is usually referred to as fundamental analysis. When fair value is established, it can be compared to the current market price to decide if the shares are a candidate for investment. An important part of fundamental analysis is the evaluation of financial statements. They consist of an income statement, a balance sheet, and a statement of cash flow.

The most widely practiced method of analysing and interpreting financial statements is by using ratios to assess operating performance, liquidity and solvency, and value indicators. An example is presented comparing fair value to market price using the earnings approach and the present value approach.

The chapter concludes with a description of special situations that suggest there may be a potential for capital gain including cash cows, thin capitalisation, new floats, small company growth, under-valued assets, changes in management or policy, hidden earnings, buybacks, and takeovers.

CHAPTER **6**

TECHNICAL ANALYSIS

So far, we have been concentrating on fundamental analysis which endeavours to determine a share's fair value. This chapter focuses on a different approach called *technical analysis* in which the emphasis is on information generated by the market itself. It uses information on past prices and trading volume to predict future price trends. At the very least, a first time investor should know enough about technical trading systems to understand the comments made by analysts. The purpose of this chapter is to survey several established technical trading systems. It begins with an explanation of the thinking behind technical analysis before going on to describe market indicators, various charting methods, moving averages and oscillators. It concludes with a discussion about using technical trading systems.

RATIONALE FOR TECHNICAL ANALYSIS

Investors who rely on technical trading systems hold the view that all the fundamentals are already built into price. Therefore, they concentrate on trying to identify a trend at an early stage to take a position that profits from it. There are several underlying assumptions that underpin technical trading systems:

- The market value of every security is determined by the interaction of supply and demand for that security.

- Supply and demand are governed by both rational and irrational investor behaviour.

- Market prices tend to move in trends that may last for some time.

- Changes in trends are the result of shifting supply and demand that can be detected in the patterns of the market prices themselves.

There are many forms of technical analysis. Some are concerned with simply identifying the direction of a trend, some try to establish the strength or momentum of a trend, while others attempt to forecast an impending reversal in a trend. There are two approaches to using technical analysis. One focuses on a subjective interpretation of chart patterns. The other focuses on an objective interpretation of the data.

Subjective technical analysis consists of interpreting the patterns that emerge from price and volume charts. The objective is to predict how the price will move by looking for areas of support and resistance. There are different types of patterns, such as flags, pennants, head and shoulders, double tops or bottoms, and many others. There are also different types of charts, including bar charts, candlestick charts, and point and figure charts. The interpretations are subjective because they depend on the judgement and experience of the individual. It is not unusual for two technical analysts to reach different conclusions about the same chart.

Objective technical analysis is more scientific because it is based on specified procedures. It is the preferred method for creating trading algorithms because they can be tested and optimised. Objective technical analysis focuses on statistical indicators instead of interpreting charts. They use the same price and volume data to assess if a stock price is trending and the strength of its momentum. Examples of popular technical indicators are simple moving averages, weighted moving averages, exponential moving averages, moving average convergence divergence indicators, relative strength oscillators, percentage range oscillators, stochastic oscillators, and many more.

Technical analysis employs a quaint terminology. A strong upward price trend is a *bull market*. A strong downward price trend is a *bear market*. When no trend is apparent, the market is going *sideways*. If the price drops briefly during a bull market, it is a *correction*. If the price rises briefly in a bear market, it is a *rally*. When the price levels off, it is variously referred to as a consolidation, congestion, or building a base. Buy and sell signals are based upon evidence of accumulation (buying) or distribution (selling).

MARKET INDICATORS

In Australia, the performance of the overall stock market is generally tracked by the S&P/ASX 200 Index. This index and others are commonly used to judge the strength of a market trend once it is underway. Three popular market indicators are the advance-decline line, the high-low index, and the pattern of trading volume.

Advance-decline line
The advance-decline line is used to assess the breadth of buying, or selling, pressure across the stock market. It consists of the number of rising shares minus the number of falling shares at the end of each day. The result of each day's advance-decline calculation is added to a cumulative total that is plotted on a chart along with the S&P/ASX 200 Index.

The advance-decline line measures whether the market is gaining or losing strength. If it follows the trend in the Index, then it is a confirmation of the trend. If the Index is rising and the advance-decline line falls, it suggests that the rising market is running out of steam. Similarly, if the Index is falling and the advance-decline line begins to rise, it suggests that selling pressure is easing and buying pressure is increasing.

High-low index

Another measure that is used to supplement or confirm the advance-decline line is the high-low index. A rising stock market will be characterised by an increasing number of shares that are reaching new highs for the year and a decreasing number of shares that are experiencing new lows for the year; the opposite occurs in a falling market.

The number of ASX shares reaching new highs for the year minus the number of shares making new lows for the year is averaged for some period, like five days. The moving average smooths out erratic daily fluctuations. The high-low index generally moves in the same direction as the market. Divergence from the market trend is a clue to a trend reversal and it can be used to confirm a similar signal from the advance-decline line.

Trading volume

Some technical analysts maintain that you cannot forecast the market strictly based on price. Trading *volume*, or the number of shares traded, is equally important because it tells us something about the strength of a change in an Index. A popular rule in technical trading systems is that volume goes with the trend. This means that in a bull market, trading volume is supposed to be strong when prices are rising and weak on corrections. In a bear market, trading volume is supposed to be strong when prices are falling and weak on rallies. Bull market peaks and bear market troughs are often characterised by diminishing volume heralding the reversal of a trend.

CHARTING TECHNIQUES

Technical analysis is an attempt to forecast future prices by studying past prices. A chart can record prices for shares, options, futures contracts, an industry average or an index. The purpose of recording prices is to establish the high and low points of investor enthusiasm with a view to anticipating future price movements.

The foundation of charting is *support* and *resistance* levels. A support level is a price at which heavy buying has typically occurred in the past. A resistance level is a price at which heavy selling has typically occurred in the past. Prices tend to 'bottom out' at support levels and 'top out' at resistance levels. Any price movement that breaks through these levels is a strong indication that a new trend has developed.

It is easy enough to record share prices and trading volume but interpreting charts correctly is more of an art than a science. False signals, whipsaws, and other errors are inevitable. Despite the shortcomings of charting, many investors use this form of technical analysis, and several charting services are offered by subscription. Three conventional types of charts are the bar chart, the candlestick chart, and the point and figure chart.

Bar chart

Perhaps the most widely used form of charting is the high-low-close bar chart. Figure 6.1 is an example of a daily bar chart. On the vertical axis is the price scale; each vertical line, or bar, connects the highest and lowest price during trading. The closing price is indicated by a cross hatch on the bar. The horizontal axis at the bottom of the chart records the time scale. The vertical lines at the bottom of the chart record the number of shares traded. Most bar charts are recorded daily, but longer-term charts are sometimes done on a weekly or monthly basis.

The key to charting is interpretation. Technical analysts look for price and volume patterns that tell them what the price is likely to do next. An important assumption in technical analysis is that once a trend is established it will persist for some time. The obvious corollary is that breaking a trend is a significant event. A bar chart provides a visual record of a price trend. A bullish chart pattern may be a decisive upside breakout from a previously established trading range or a price that is holding above a previously established resistance level. A bearish chart pattern may be a decisive downside breakout from a previously established trading range or a price that is falling away from a previously established support level.

Figure 6.1 Daily bar chart

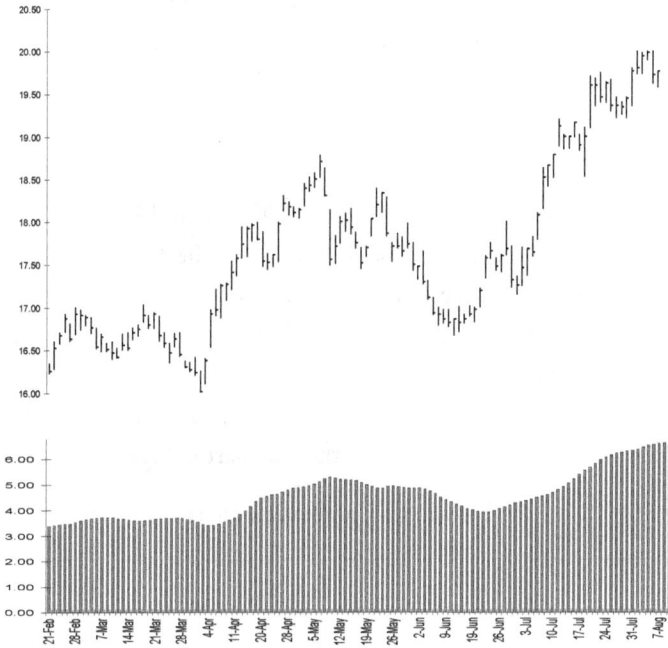

Heavy volume is interpreted as strength in the underlying trend, whereas light volume is interpreted as weakness in the underlying trend. A rising price on increasing volume is an indication of a continuing up-trend, while a falling price on increasing volume is an indication of a continuing down-trend. A rising price on light volume is an indication that the up-trend is weak, and a falling price on light volume is an indication that the down-trend may soon reverse.

The bar chart in Figure 6.1 begins with a period of consolidation on light volume between a support level at $16.00 and a resistance level at $17.00. There is a strong upside breakout through the $17.00 resistance level on rising volume signalling

93

an upward trend. The price reaches $18.50 before a correction back to $17.00 on decreasing volume. Then the trend resumes with a strong recovery on heavy volume to reach $20.00. The record of past prices is clear. The technical analyst's challenge is to predict what will happen next.

Candlestick chart

The candlestick charting system uses the open, high, low and closing prices in a way that is similar to the bar chart. The difference is that the bar is now a candlestick. The candlestick is filled in when the closing price is below the opening price, and it is left open when the closing price is above the opening price. The candlesticks help to identify strength and weakness. Figure 6.2 is the candlestick version of the bar chart in Figure 6.1

Figure 6.2 Candlestick chart

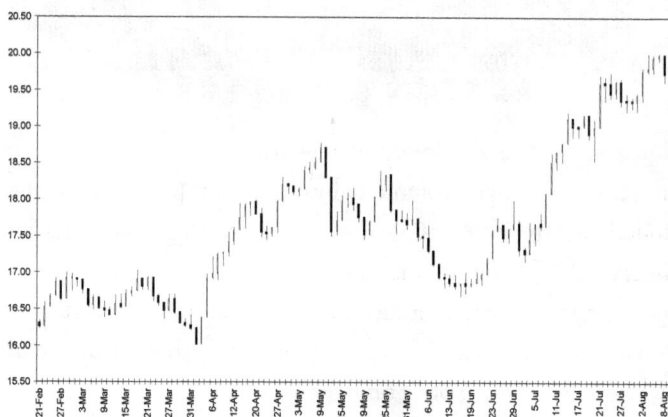

Point and figure chart

The proponents of point and figure charts contend that market prices spend the majority of the time going sideways. The point and figure chart condenses the sideways movements and focuses more clearly on the important rises and falls. Consequently, support and resistance patterns are easier to identify and important buy and sell signals are easier to recognise.

Point and figure charts do this by dispensing with the time axis. In this way, they capture each significant price movement regardless of how long it takes to occur. These charts also ignore trading volume. According to point and figure chartists, when the price breaks out of a horizontal trading range, it will continue vertically for the same distance that it went across. This process of determining the extent of a rise or a fall is known as the count. Figure 6.3 is the point and figure equivalent of the previous examples.

Figure 6.3 Point and figure chart

20.00																
19.80																X
19.60													X		X	X
19.40													X	O		O
19.20													X			
19.00												X	X			
18.80												X	O			
18.60			X									X				
18.40			X	O		X						X				
18.20			X	O		X	O					X				
18.00			X	O	X	X	O					X				
17.80		X	X	O	X	O	X	O				X				
17.60		X	O	X	O	X	O	X	O	X		X				
17.40		X	O		O		O		O	X	O	X				
17.20		X							O	X	O					
17.00	X	X							O	X						
16.80	X	O	X						O							
16.60	X	O	X													
16.40	X	O	X													
16.20	X	O	X													
16.00		O														
15.80																

There are two elements that need to be selected for a point and figure chart. The first element is the scale on the vertical price axis which is the box size. The box size is usually smaller for short-term trading and larger for longer-term trading. In the example, the box size is 20 cents. The second element is the reversal size. This is the number of boxes that the price must reverse before we begin a new column. In the example, the reversal size is one box. The conventional symbols are **X** in rising columns and **O** in falling columns. Course of sales price data are ideal for point and figure charting.

MOVING AVERAGES

A moving average of past prices can be used as an indicator of a price trend. A simple moving average is calculated by adding together the closing prices during the averaging period and dividing by the number of trading days. An alternative to the simple moving average is the weighted moving average in which recent prices are given greater weight so that the moving average will be more representative of the current market trend. Some chartists prefer the exponential moving average because it produces a smoother line. Figure 6.4 is an example of two simple moving averages superimposed over the bar chart from Figure 6.1. The thick line is a 35-day moving average and the thin line is a 10-day moving average.

Finding the right number of days to use in the averaging period is important. Long-term investors often use a 200-day moving average, whereas short-term investors may prefer a 5-day moving average. Since it is a cumulative indicator, the longer the averaging period, the more sluggish a moving average will be. If you want a more sensitive moving average, make it shorter.

However, a very short moving average can be too sensitive causing it to *whipsaw* resulting in many false signals. A buy signal is given when the price moves through the moving average from below. A sell signal is given when the price moves through the moving average from above.

Figure 6.4 Moving averages

The Moving Average Convergence Divergence indicator (MACD) is another way to use moving averages. It is a way of comparing the short-term trend with the long-term trend by plotting a long-term moving average together with a short-term moving average. In Figure 6.4, the long-term trend is represented by the 35-day moving average and the short-term trend is represented by the 10-day moving average. The shorter-period moving average always fluctuates more markedly than the longer-period one. A buy signal is given when the short-term moving average crosses over the long-term moving average from below. A sell signal is given when the short-term moving average crosses over the long-term moving average from above.

OSCILLATORS

Charts and moving averages tell us something about the trend. An oscillator is a tool that measures *momentum* or the rate of change in price movement. Its purpose is to identify over-bought and over-sold conditions. These conditions occur when momentum slows down near a top or bottom and the trend is getting ready to reverse direction. There are several versions of the oscillator including the relative strength oscillator, the percentage range oscillator, and the stochastic oscillator.

The relative strength oscillator is a measure of the rate of change in price movement. The rate of change can be either accelerating or decelerating and it is expressed as a percentage. If the relative strength oscillator moves above 80 percent, it is considered over-bought and a top is forecast. If the relative strength oscillator goes below 20 percent, it is considered over-sold and a bottom is forecast.

The percentage range oscillator calculates the position of the closing price within its range over some period. When it goes below 20 percent it is considered over-bought and a top is forecast. When it goes above 80 percent it is considered over-sold and a bottom is forecast. A sudden move from one extreme to the other is an indication that a complete change in direction is beginning. Alternatively, a price movement that is not accompanied by a strong percentage range indicates that the move may not have the momentum to carry it much further.

The stochastic oscillator is also based on the premise that prices tend to accumulate near the upper end of their trading range in a rising market and near the lower end of their trading range in a falling market. When the stochastic oscillator goes above 80 percent, it is considered over-bought and a top is forecast. When the stochastic oscillator goes under 20 percent it is considered over-sold and a bottom is forecast. However, in a strongly trending market the stochastic oscillator may remain in these extreme areas for some time.

USING TECHNICAL TRADING SYSTEMS

Technical analysis can be a labour intensive activity because there are hundreds of stocks that you can follow and scores of complex technical trading systems. With the availability of technical trading systems online, private investors have the same capacity to engage in technical analysis as professional traders. Online stockbroker websites are usually the first place to look for technical trading information that is free. There are also technical trading websites that are available by subscription. Some are designed to produce charts quickly and easily so the user may make their own interpretation. Others go a step further by calculating several technical indicators. A few go even further by invoking a set of specified trading rules that automatically produce buy and sell signals. Websites that include more features are generally more expensive and a good knowledge of technical analysis is important if you want to get the best results from these websites. Paying for the subscription is only the first step, you also need to know how to use this information to get your money's worth. Here are a few examples.

- MetaStock at **metastock.com**
- OmniTrader at **omnitrader.com**
- SuperCharts at **eoddata.com**
- Advanced GET at **esignal.com**
- TradeStation at **tradestation.com**
- EzyChart at **ezychart.com**
- Pro Trader at **protradercharts.com**
- Bullcharts at **bullcharts.com.au**

If you decide to adopt technical analysis, you will come across an array of patterns and indicators with rules to match. For example, a sell signal is given when the short-term moving average crosses the long-term moving average from above. Even though this is a rule, it is not steadfast and can be subject to other factors such as volume and momentum. Similarly, what works for one stock may not work for another. A 50-day moving average may work to identify trends for one stock but a 70-day moving average may be better for another.

One thing is for certain, there is no question about the current price of a share. After all, it is available for all to see, and nobody doubts its legitimacy. The price set by the market reflects the sum of the knowledge of all the participants and many of them are very sophisticated investors. They have considered everything they know about a share and settled on a decision about whether to buy, hold, sell, or avoid it. These are the forces of supply and demand at work. By examining price action to determine which force is prevailing, technical analysis focuses directly on the current market price, where it has been, and where it may be going. Even though there are some universal principles and rules that can be applied, technical analysis is more of an art than a science and, as an art form, it is widely subject to interpretation.

ARTIFICIAL INTELLIGENCE

Identifying the exact means by which a technical trading system can be profitably exploited is like searching for the holy grail of investing. The reason this type of analysis can be so elusive is because technical trading systems must deal with factors that are difficult to pin down.

- Technical trading variables are constantly changing and trading rules that worked in the past do not necessarily work in the future.

- Technical trading variables do not act in isolation, as they change, they have an impact on other variables around them.

- When a variable cannot be expressed in the form of a simple straight line it is 'non-linear' and this is a complicating condition with technical trading variables.

- The interpretation of technical trading systems is not always apparent, and sometimes they produce frustratingly vague or ambiguous signals.

- The number of possible combinations of variables involved in constructing a trading system can be overwhelming.

A different approach to evaluating problems with these features has been to employ artificial intelligence techniques including *neural networks* and *genetic algorithms*. Some are available on subscription websites and others are software packages that run on your personal computer. They have been used in a variety of applications including stock price forecasting, stock selection, exchange rate forecasting, index forecasting, interest rate forecasting, and futures trading.

Neural network

A neural network allows the data itself to determine both the structure and the parameters of a trading system. It learns by example and adapts itself using a process of performance feedback. It is based on the same processes that go on in the human brain to solve complex tasks such as visual pattern recognition or learning a language. Creating a neural network consists of configuring the network and training it.

A neural network is made up of neurons that are organised into layers. The first layer consists of the input neurons. The last layer consists of the output neurons. In between, there are one or more hidden layers. Each neuron in a layer receives signals from all the neurons in the previous layer. Both the number of layers and the number of neurons in each layer need to be configured. Different configurations can be used for the same problem.

A neural network learns by using either a feed-back system or a feed-forward system. In a feed-back system, the results of the output neurons are fed back into the input neurons until the neural network becomes stable. In a feed-forward system, the network is trained using many examples of input variables with known results. Training a network usually requires many runs through training data as the system adaptively adjusts the weights between each of the neuron connections. Training is completed when the error rate falls below a specified tolerance level.

The result is a neural network that has learned the optimal combination of complex variables in predicting a specific outcome. It decides for itself which input variables are important and in what combination they are used to make a prediction. When it receives new data, it produces a judgement by firing one or more of the output neurons. It is pure black box forecasting. It derives its forecasting powers by trial-and-error and it cannot actually tell us how the forecasts work. Some neural networks perform better than others and the art of building good ones appears to be the way in which they are configured and trained.

Genetic algorithm
Genetic algorithms differ from neural networks because they not only deliver information about how to trade, but also why. Genetic algorithms are based on a computer simulation of Darwinian evolution theory. Each generation consists of several individuals of varying fitness or ability to perform. The chance of an individual surviving to the next generation is proportional to its fitness.

The parallel in stockmarket forecasting is that every trading rule has a certain fitness in terms of its ability to contribute to a correct prediction. Over successive generations the stronger trading rules will survive, and the weaker ones will not. The genetic algorithm consists of a computer program that creates an environment in which trading rules compete and only the fittest survive. It generates and evaluates every possible trading rule associated with a particular data set and then combines the best ones together. By repeating this process many times, it evolves a trading system consisting of the strongest predictive variables in the correct combination.

By generating and testing a wide variety of trading scenarios, the genetic algorithm avoids the inflexibility traditionally associated with technical trading systems. Each trading scenario can compete with every other trading scenario, and it is not easily distracted by the occasional disruptive influences that occur in financial markets. The forecasting effectiveness of genetic algorithms is still being explored. Its searching skills may help to unearth neglected or previously undiscovered technical trading systems.

SUMMARY

Technical analysis uses information on past prices and trading volume to predict future price trends. There are many forms of technical analysis. Some are concerned with simply identifying the direction of a trend. Some try to establish the strength or momentum of a trend. Others attempt to forecast an impending reversal in a trend. There are two approaches to using technical analysis. Subjective technical analysis consists of interpreting the patterns that emerge from price and volume charts. There are different types of charts including bar charts, candlestick charts, and point and figure charts. Objective technical analysis focuses on statistical indicators instead of interpreting charts. Examples include moving averages, moving average convergence divergence indicators, relative strength oscillators, percentage range oscillators, and stochastic oscillators. Online stockbroker websites are usually the first place to look for technical trading information that is free. There are also technical trading websites that are available by subscription. A different approach to technical analysis employs artificial intelligence. Two examples are neural networks and genetic algorithms.

Part C

STARTING OUT IN MANAGED INVESTMENTS

Managed investments are another starting point for some first time investors. A managed investment is a pool of funds that is professionally administered on behalf of individual investors. It is a means by which individuals can invest indirectly in shares, interest bearing securities, property, and other assets. In Australia, there has been a dramatic expansion of managed investments partly because of the massive increase in superannuation savings and partly as a result of improvements in how private investors can access them.

Fund managers are skilled professionals whose objective is to enhance the wealth of investors. They undertake the process of selecting investments and when to trade. They have access to the resources needed to research and analyse individual investments, gauge economic trends, and make investment decisions. They offer economies of scale and diversification through a single investment. They make no promises, however, about the results they will achieve on behalf of investors. Managed investments have advantages and disadvantages. The purpose of Part C is to help you determine if managed investments should play a part in your investment program.

CHAPTER **7**

FEATURES OF MANAGED INVESTMENTS

The managed investments industry consists of a diverse group of institutions offering a variety of investment products. The managed funds market is divided into a wholesale sector and a retail sector. The wholesale sector promotes itself to superannuation funds, government agencies, and others that can meet their minimum required investment. The retail sector serves individual or personal investors and accommodates minimum investments of as little as $500. The purpose of this chapter is to examine the retail sector for managed investments. It explores reasons for and against investing in a managed fund, the range of managed fund products, and the function of the product disclosure statement.

PROS AND CONS OF MANAGED INVESTMENTS

Is it better to put your money under professional management or invest it yourself? According to an ASX share ownership survey, approximately 40 percent of Australian adults own shares either directly or indirectly. About 15 percent invest directly, 12 percent invest indirectly, and 13 percent invest both directly and indirectly. What this means is there is no clear consensus among Australian investors about the best way to invest.

Some first time investors prefer managed investments because they do not have enough confidence to make their own investment decisions. They expect a managed investment to provide them with greater safety and less personal involvement than direct investing. The benefits include professional expertise, diversification, and less demand on your time. The drawbacks include extra costs and average performance. Choosing to invest indirectly depends on how you view the tradeoff between the investment performance you want and the amount of effort you are prepared to put into it.

Professional fund managers have a great deal of investment expertise. They have the capacity to research numerous investment opportunities. They have the tools to analyse economic and financial information, make asset allocation decisions and monitor a portfolio that matches a set of investment objectives. An individual investor is unlikely to have the same time, resources, or expertise. Managed funds provide smaller investors with a measure of risk protection. A large portfolio is diversified, whereas a small investor may not be able to achieve a significant degree of diversification. Large funds can also use options, futures and other hedging devices that are not easily available to smaller investors. Owning shares in companies in the United States, Asia, or Europe, introduces additional complications for private investors and international investing is much easier through a managed fund.

The advantages of managed funds come at a cost. The track record for most managed funds suggests they do not consistently produce returns that are any better than the market average for their asset class. Moreover, managed funds impose a variety of fees that reduce the returns to investors. The prospect of average performance combined with extra costs puts a spotlight on whether a managed fund will be suited to your investment objectives.

SINGLE ASSET FUNDS

A managed fund has a set of objectives that guide the way in which it operates. These objectives form the foundation for the fund manager's investment strategy. There are a variety of funds that only invest in a single asset class.

A cash management fund is an attractive alternative to holding short-term deposits in bank accounts that earn little or no interest. They invest in short-term money market securities such as bank accepted bills, treasury notes and interest-bearing deposits. The maturity period for most investments is less than 90 days, so they closely track the yields in the short-term money market. An investment in a cash management fund is virtually at call.

A capital guaranteed fund may invest in the full range of assets but generally limits the portfolio to fixed income securities. The returns are modest but the original investment plus declared earnings are guaranteed. This type of fund is particularly suitable for cautious investors who want security of their capital or who have a short investment horizon.

Fixed income funds invest in securities issued or guaranteed by the Commonwealth, state or local governments and their statutory authorities as well as corporate fixed income securities, mortgages, and preference shares. The maturity of fixed income fund investments is generally medium to long-term. Their objectives are a high interest yield with some profit from trading activity because of changes in interest rates.

Mortgage funds loan money on secured and registered first mortgages over real estate. They also invest in some fixed income securities for liquidity. The interest rates on the mortgages may be fixed or variable. The returns from mortgage funds tend to be more stable than cash management funds and fixed income funds. Short-term fluctuations in interest rates also have less impact.

Property funds differ according to the type of property (commercial, retail, industrial, residential or tourism) and its location (central business district, outer urban growth area or suburban shopping centre). Property funds have an income component and a growth component. If the fund borrows to maximise growth, then the income component will be reduced to pay the interest on the borrowings. Depending on the manager's strategy, a property fund may target high income and low growth, balanced income and growth, or low income and high growth. A split property fund offers separate income and growth investments.

Australian equity funds generally invest in listed Australian shares. The investment strategies pursued by individual funds varies enormously. Equity funds that emphasise growth take on greater risk by investing in industry sectors like resources or concentrating on things like special situations. Equity funds that emphasise income stick to high-yielding *blue chip* shares, shares paying fully franked dividends, and preference shares. Different kinds of managed investments can be found among equity funds.

- Industrial funds invest in the larger Australian industrial shares with a view to steady growth over the longer term.
- Resource funds invest in the shares of mining and petroleum companies with a view to strong growth over the longer term.

- Small cap funds (small capitalisation) invest in the shares of smaller companies with a view to strong potential growth.

- Special situation funds invest in the shares of companies that are in circumstances that may lead to a capital gain such as a takeover.

- Imputation funds invest in companies that pay fully franked dividends.

- Index funds invest in a selection of shares that replicate the performance of a stockmarket index like the S&P/ASX 200 Index.

Funds that invest in overseas companies are generally managed locally by a fund manager with international links. The globalisation of securities' markets together with the advantages of international diversification have increased the popularity of overseas funds. Overseas funds invest in fixed income securities, shares, property, and currencies. Overseas funds may spread their investments around the world, or they may target specific regions such as America, Europe, Japan, or the Pacific basin. Overseas funds carry the additional risk of changes in the exchange rate between the Australian dollar and the currencies in which overseas investments are made. Most of this risk can be hedged. For these reasons, the expenses associated with managing international investments are higher.

DIVERSIFIED FUNDS

Diversified funds invest in the full range of asset classes including money market securities, fixed income securities, property, and shares. Diversified funds are usually characterised as stable funds, balanced funds, growth funds, or hedge funds.

Stable funds are designed to achieve a reasonable level of capital stability. Capital stability means minimising the chance of negative returns. They range from cash funds that invest in short term money market securities and fixed income securities to conservative funds with up to 30 percent in shares and property. Investors in a stable fund expect modest returns over the short term with relatively low risk.

Balanced funds may have investments in shares, property, fixed income and money market securities. The proportions vary considerably depending on the fund manager's views on timing and asset allocation. Exposure to shares is usually limited to 50 percent of the portfolio. Investors in a balanced fund expect a moderate return over the medium term with the possibility that there may be a negative return in some years.

Growth funds concentrate up to 85 percent of the portfolio in shares and property with the remainder in cash or fixed income securities for liquidity purposes. Investors in growth funds expect superior returns over the longer term. However, they are also exposed to greater risk and are more likely to experience negative returns in some years.

Hedge funds invest in a variety of assets. Their main claim is they are managed so that their returns are not correlated to returns in other investment products or the market. They achieve this by diversification and a range of hedging devices such as short selling, options, futures, and warrants. A hedge fund's objective is to maximise investor returns and eliminate risk. However, they are more aggressive and therefore riskier than growth funds.

EXCHANGE TRADED FUNDS (ETF)

You can buy and sell ETF units through a stockbroker in the same way you buy and sell shares. When you invest in an ETF you don't own the underlying assets, you own units in the ETF and the ETF owns the underlying investments. Most ETFs in Australia are passively managed which means they usually have lower management fees than actively managed funds. They track a particular asset class or market index such as Australian shares, international shares, sector shares like resources or financials, fixed income securities, commodities and metals, foreign currencies, market indices like the S&P/ASX 200 Index, and many others.

ETFs enable a private investor to invest in a basket of the underlying assets with a single transaction. This offers diversification within an asset class, and diversification across asset classes by investing in more than one ETF. They publish their net asset value daily on the ASX website as well as on their own websites. Net asset value represents the underlying portfolio value of a unit, and this is used to follow the fund's performance.

ETFs are *open-ended* which means that additional units are created when there are more buyers than sellers and units are redeemed when there are more sellers than buyers. One benefit of this arrangement is liquidity that enables investors to buy and sell easily. The price of a unit is not determined by supply and demand, rather it is tied to the net asset value of the underlying portfolio. If the value of the underlying portfolio increases, then the price of a unit also increases. If the value of the underlying portfolio falls, then so does the price of the units. You can visit the ASX at *asxetfs.com* for a list of the ETFs that are available and check out the individual ETF websites for more information.

LISTED INVESTMENT COMPANIES (LIC)

LICs are incorporated as a company and their shares are listed on an exchange. You can buy and sell shares in a LIC through your stockbroker. When you invest in a LIC you don't own the underlying assets, you own shares in the LIC and the LIC owns the underlying investments. LICs are *closed-end* funds which means they have a fixed number of shares and, unlike an ETF, they don't normally issue new shares or cancel existing shares. The price of LIC shares, therefore, fluctuates because of supply and demand in the market. The shares of LICs tend to trade at a discount from net asset value, and some are thinly traded which means it may not always be easy to complete a transaction. As a company, a LIC may pay dividends at the discretion of the directors. Visit the ASX website at **asxlics.com** for a list of LICs and visit their individual websites for more information.

Most LICs in Australia are actively managed which means they are seeking greater returns than passively managed funds. It also means they have higher management fees than passively managed funds. They generally invest in listed Australian shares, international shares, and some industry sectors. There are a few LICs that employ aggressive strategies that include short selling, options, futures, and leverage. Listed investment trusts (LITs) are like LICs except they are incorporated as a trust. They are closed-end funds in which trust units can be bought and sold on an exchange through a stockbroker. LITs pay out any surplus income to investors as trust distributions.

UNLISTED MANAGED FUNDS

Unlisted managed funds are incorporated as unit trusts and are not traded on an exchange. The fund manager promotes the sale of units through intermediaries and manages the fund according to a constitution that sets down the rights, responsibilities, policies and procedures. The manager must be a corporation and must have a securities dealer's license issued by the ASIC. A third party acts as custodian of the trust assets on behalf of the unit holders. The law requires the manager to provide regular reports to the unit holders including a review of the investment operations and the financial details of the trust.

Unlisted managed funds cover every type of investment strategy. They invest in a broad spectrum of asset classes such as Australian shares, international shares, fixed income securities, and real estate. In addition to specialising in a particular asset class, they may invest according to a variety of different styles and techniques. The price of a unit depends upon its net asset value which fluctuates according to changes in the value of the underlying portfolio. Unlisted trusts are *open-end* funds providing a continuous offering and redemption of units.

There are several ways you can invest in an unlisted managed fund. If you want to deal directly, you send an application to the fund manager that you download from their website. If you want to use an intermediary, stockbrokers and licensed financial advisers can process your order. You can also buy and sell units in some unlisted funds in the same way you buy and sell shares using an online stockbroker and the ASX mFund service. Unlisted managed funds tend to have higher fees and they may have restrictions on how you can withdraw your money. For example, some funds require you to keep your investment for a minimum of 12 months before you can withdraw part or all of it.

SUPERANNUATION FUNDS

The spectacular growth in managed funds has been largely driven by the universal and mandatory Australian superannuation scheme. A Superannuation fund is a unit trust that is designed specifically to comply with superannuation legislation. It can receive employer and employee contributions, rollover payments from other superannuation funds, and eligible termination payments from leaving a job. Superannuation is a long-term investment that cannot normally be withdrawn until you retire. Benefits can be paid as a lump sum or as a pension. There are five categories of superannuation funds.

- Corporate funds are sponsored by a single employer or a group of related employers.
- Industry funds are sponsored by unions and employer organisations that originated from earlier industrial workplace arrangements.
- Public sector funds provide benefits for government employees.
- Retail funds are publicly offered superannuation funds that you join by purchasing units.
- Self-managed superannuation funds (SMSFs) are used by individuals or family members who want to exercise greater control over their investments and greater flexibility in tax planning.

Accumulation products

Accumulation products accept superannuation contributions and invest them until you retire. They are designed to take advantage of tax concessions for people who are saving for their retirement. You can transfer your money between different investment options within a fund, and you can transfer your money to another super fund at any time (called a rollover). However, you cannot normally withdraw your money until you reach retirement age.

Employer contributions are based on a percentage of your earnings. You can also make your own voluntary contributions. Concessional voluntary contributions are made to your super account pre-tax such as a salary sacrifice arrangement with your employer, and you can make non-concessional voluntary contributions after tax from your own funds. The government can also make a co-contribution if you earn less than a certain amount and make a voluntary contribution into your account.

Once your superannuation fund receives your employer contributions and any voluntary contributions you have decided to make, it invests this money into an investment option that you have chosen. If you have not chosen one of its investment options, the contributions will be invested in a default option called MySuper. Most super funds provide several options that offer different risk and return profiles. Fund managers have various names for their investment options. For diversified funds they usually boil down to five categories:

- Conservative funds aim to achieve returns in excess of inflation with low risk by investing mostly in defensive assets such as cash and fixed income securities. They are aimed at those who are risk adverse and/or in retirement.

- Moderate funds aim to achieve modest returns by investing around 40 percent in growth assets and 60 percent in defensive assets with low to medium risk. They are usually aimed at those who are nearing retirement.

- Balanced funds aim to achieve average returns by investing around 60 percent in growth assets and 40 percent in defensive assets with medium risk. They are usually aimed at those who are in the middle of their working life. This is also the MySuper option.

- Growth funds aim to achieve high long-term returns by investing up to 80 percent in growth assets and limiting their investment in defensive assets. They are aimed at those who are willing to accept a higher level of risk in the expectation of higher returns.

- Aggressive funds aim to achieve very high long-term returns by investing mostly in growth assets and very little in defensive assets. They can be subject to significant volatility on a year-to-year basis. They are aimed at those with a higher risk appetite.

In addition to diversified options, many superannuation funds offer investment options in specific asset classes such as fixed income securities, large company shares, small company shares, or international shares. There are also funds that offer options based on themes such as a particular industry sector or ethical investments based on environmental principles.

Allocated products

Allocated superannuation products are post-retirement products. Also called an account-based pension, it enables you to transition your superannuation into a pension account so that you not only have a regular income, but also defer the tax on investment earnings that might otherwise be paid. To receive the tax concessions, you need to comply with minimum and maximum pension payments prescribed by the Government.

The pension payments consist of investment earnings and some return of your capital. One of the features that makes allocated products attractive is the degree of control you retain. For example, you can continue to specify the option(s) in which you want your money invested, you can elect to take a partial lump sum withdrawal at any time, and you can vary the pension payments within the minimum and maximum limits. The balance in your account depends on investment earnings, lump sum withdrawals and pension payments. The benefits continue if there are funds in the account.

Self-managed superannuation fund (SMSF)

Do-it-yourself or self-managed superannuation funds are the fastest growing segment of the superannuation industry. Running your own superannuation fund involves a tremendous amount of effort and expense to comply with the SMSF regulations. However, the cost may be rewarded in terms of tax savings and control over your retirement investments. You should seek expert advice on self-managed superannuation because it is not only complicated, but also subject to legislative changes by the Commonwealth government.

PRODUCT DISCLOSURE STATEMENT

The Product Disclosure Statement is potentially the most important piece of information you have to judge a managed investment. It explains the fund's investment objectives, who manages the fund, past performance, the fees they charge and more. It is a legal requirement that you are given a Product Disclosure Statement before you invest.

When you read it, look for information that will help you decide if this fund meets your investment criteria.

- What are the fund's investment objectives? Do they align with your investment objectives? What methods are used to achieve the investment objective? Is it actively or passively managed?

- What are the significant risks associated with investing in the fund? Do they align with your tolerance for risk?

- What is the minimum investment amount? Can additional units be purchased in smaller increments?

- What is the nature and frequency of income and capital gains distributions?

- What fees and costs are charged including establishment fees, contribution fees, withdrawal fees, management fees, and performance fees.

- How can I withdraw my investment? What notice is required to withdraw an investment and what determines the price I will receive?

SUMMARY

A managed investment is a pool of funds that is professionally administered on behalf of individual investors. There are arguments for and against investing in managed funds. The benefits include professional expertise, diversification, and less demand on your time. The drawbacks include extra costs and average performance. It depends on how you view the tradeoff between the investment performance you want and the amount of effort you are prepared to put into it.

There are single asset funds such as cash management funds, fixed income funds, mortgage funds, property funds, Australian equity funds and overseas funds. There are also diversified funds that invest in the full range of asset classes including stable funds, balanced funds, growth funds and hedge funds. Managed investment products available for retail investors in Australia include Exchange Traded Funds (ETFs), Listed Investment Companies (LICs), unlisted managed funds and superannuation funds.

It is a legal requirement that you are given a Product Disclosure Statement before you invest that explains the fund's objectives, who manages the fund, past performance, the fees they charge, and other information about the fund.

CHAPTER 8

PERFORMANCE OF MANAGED INVESTMENTS

The main reason why some first time investors are attracted to managed investments is because they expect the fund manager to perform better than they would as direct investors. Unfortunately, investors expect more than fund managers can usually deliver. Very few investment managers consistently beat the market over the longer term and past performance has been shown not to be a good indicator of future performance. Moreover, the fees charged for a managed investment can amount to a significant reduction in your returns. This chapter considers the pros and cons of active versus passive funds management, the impact of fees charged by managed funds, how to monitor the performance of managed funds, and the track record for actively managed funds in Australia.

ACTIVE VERSUS PASSIVE FUND MANAGEMENT

If you choose to invest in a managed fund, one of your first decisions is whether you want one that is passively managed or actively managed. Knowing the potential advantages and disadvantages of each approach will help you determine which best matches your investment objectives.

Passive fund management is essentially a buy-and-hold approach, and the main advantage is low fees. The fees are lower because there is no requirement to actively manage the investments. The fund manager maintains a predetermined mix of investments and they do not normally make adjustments even if certain sectors or companies are underperforming. A popular version of a passively managed fund is the index fund. The fund manager does not try to beat the benchmark index. Instead, they pick a representative sample of investments that track the index. The logic behind an index fund is that matching the average returns of a benchmark index and operating at a lower cost will produce overall results that are comparable to an actively managed fund.

The aim of active fund management is to beat the market or outperform a particular benchmark. Active fund managers not only have a greater range of investments to choose from, but they can also engage in short-term trading opportunities. Active fund managers are able to control their exposure to risk by avoiding or selling underperforming investments and they can use short sales, put options and other strategies to hedge against risk. If an active fund manager makes good investment decisions, you could potentially see greater returns than you would with a passively managed fund. On the other hand, if an active fund manager makes poor choices, you could lose more money than with a passively managed fund.

IMPACT OF FEES

Compared with direct investing, managed investments incur additional costs. Read the Product Disclosure Statement provided by the fund manager for full details about which fees apply and how they may affect your returns.

Exchange traded funds

You pay stockbroker fees whenever you buy or sell ETF units which vary depending on your stockbroker. The bid-ask spread is an additional transaction cost when you invest in ETF units. You buy an ETF unit at the higher *ask price* and sell an ETF unit at the lower *bid price*. The market maker buys at the bid price and sells at the ask price. The difference between these two, the *bid-ask spread*, is a transaction cost in addition to the brokerage fees. It is essentially a fee charged by the market maker as compensation for providing the liquidity to enable trading in an ETF.

ETFs charge management fees that typically range between 0.1 and 1 percent of net assets annually. They are lower for passively managed ETFs and higher for actively managed ETFs. ETFs generally have the lowest management fees compared with other types of managed investments. Management fees are levied regardless of an ETF's performance.

Listed invest companies

Brokerage fees also apply whenever you buy or sell shares in a LIC. The buy/sell spread also adds to the cost of trading in LICs. Most LICs are actively managed, and their management fees typically range from 1 to 1.5 percent of net assets annually. Management fees are levied regardless of how well a LIC performs. If the fund manager outperforms a specified benchmark, some funds also charge a performance fee. The amount varies, but 10 to 20 percent of the outperformance is common. The performance fee may be payable even if the fund makes a negative return if the return is above the benchmark. Not all LICs charge a performance fee. Overall fees for LICs are typically higher than for ETFs but lower than for unlisted funds.

Unlisted funds

Some unlisted funds charge an entry fee, sometimes known as an establishment fee, a front-end fee, or a contribution fee, that may be as high as 5 percent of the amount invested. A substantial part of the entry fee is paid as a commission to the brokers, financial advisers and financial planners who sell managed investments. The entry fee has been a big problem for the managed investments industry. It deters many investors from putting their money under management. For this reason, there are many 'no-load' funds that have no entry fee. However, watch out for no-load funds that try to claw back the entry fee with higher management fees and exit fees. A fund manager may also be paying out a trailing commission from your account of 1 to 2 percent per year to the intermediary who sold you units in the fund. There have been some funds that charge an entry fee and a trailing commission even when you invest directly with them.

Management fees are regularly deducted from each account. There is also the recovery of running costs such as auditors' fees, trustee fees, custodian fees, interest expense, bank charges, postage, and printing. The overall cost of operating a managed investment is measured by the management expense ratio (MER). It consists of the annual management fees and the recoverable expenses paid out of the fund expressed as a percentage of the fund's average value. MERs for retail funds in Australia typically range from 0.5 percent to 3 percent with the average closer to 2 percent. Management fees are payable no matter how well the fund performs. There is no evidence that funds with higher MERs consistently deliver better performance. Some funds allow the manager to charge a performance fee if the return is better than the benchmark or target return.

To redeem units in an unlisted fund, the unit holder sends an application to the fund manager who is obliged to buy the units back within a prescribed time. Some funds charge an exit fee that can be as high as 5 percent. Others charge an exit fee based on a sliding scale depending on how long your money was under management. Many funds do not charge an exit fee.

Superannuation funds

The fees charged by a superannuation fund generally depend on the type of fund, the investment option you have selected, and the balance of your account. Industry superannuation funds generally charge members lower fees compared with retail superannuation funds. Industry super funds don't pay commissions to intermediaries and their profits are returned to the members. Retail superannuation funds are typically run by financial institutions who retain some of the profit before making distributions to the members. The ongoing fees for retail super funds typically average around 1.1 percent whereas the ongoing fees for industry super funds average around 0.6 percent. There is a range of possible fees that could be charged to a superannuation account.

- Administration fee – a general ongoing fee as either a fixed fee or a percentage of an account balance to cover the general cost of managing a super account.

- Establishment fee – a fee to set up a super account.

- Investment fee – an ongoing fee to cover the costs associated with making investments. It is usually charged as a percentage of an account and it can vary depending on the choice of investment options.

- Performance fee – a fee calculated as percentage of the investment returns that exceed a certain benchmark.

- Switching fee – a fee that may be charged if you switch investment options within the same fund. Some funds charge a buy/sell spread fee instead of a switching fee.
- Buy/sell spread fee – the same thing as a bid/ask spread. Whenever you make contributions, withdrawals, or switch investment options, it is the difference between the buying price and the selling price for the fund's units.
- Financial advice fee – A fee that may be charged if you access superannuation-related financial advice through your super fund.
- Trailing commissions – ongoing fees paid to financial intermediaries who sell superannuation products.

The reason why fees are an important consideration in selecting a superannuation fund is because your money is invested for your entire working life. Higher fees have a significant effect on the funds available when you retire.

Effect of fees on returns

The fees associated with managed investments affect the returns to investors. Figure 8.1 shows the impact of fees on the accumulated value of $10 000 invested at the beginning of each year for 30 years. It assumes that the fund earns 8 percent annually before management expenses. The initial entry fee in the left column ranges from 0 to 5 percent. The annual management expense ratio ranges from 0.5 to 2.5 percent. The accumulated value depends on the entry fee and the management expense ratio. The difference between the highest cost fund (5.0 percent entry fee and 2.5 percent MER) and the lowest cost fund (no entry fee and 0.5 percent MER) is one-third of the accumulated value at the end of 30 years.

Figure 8.1 Fees and accumulated value

Entry Fee	Management Expense Ratio				
	0.5%	1.0%	1.5%	2.0%	2.5%
0.0%	1 033 985	944 600	863 742	790 576	724 350
1.0%	1 023 645	935 154	855 105	782 670	717 106
2.0%	1 013 305	925 708	846 467	774 764	709 863
3.0%	1 002 965	916 262	837 830	766 859	702 619
4.0%	992 626	906 816	829 192	758 953	695 376
5.0%	982 286	897 370	820 555	751 047	688 132

If a fund charges an exit fee, then the accumulated value is further reduced. For example, if the no load fund with an accumulated value of $1 033 985 charges a 5 percent exit fee, then the redemption value is reduced to $982 286. This is the same redemption value that would occur for a fund that charged a 5 percent entry fee and no exit fee.

Taxation

Taxation is a cost that also affects the returns from managed investments. ETFs, LITs and unlisted funds are unit trusts. They are not a tax entity and pay no tax themselves. They distribute their income and capital gains to the unit holders who pay tax on them. A unit trust can also pass on tax credits such as dividend imputation credits or depreciation benefits from property investments.

LICs pay company tax on their income and capital gains before the Board of Directors decides what dividends will be paid to shareholders. This means LIC investors may be able to receive fully franked dividends. LICs tend to have higher portfolio turnover than ETFs, which creates an ongoing 'tax drag' from realising more capital gains each year.

MONITERING PERFORMANCE

Investors in managed funds need to be able to monitor their investments. There are several sources of information about the performance of managed investments including account statements, fund reports, and research organisation websites.

Account statement

The most important source of performance information is your account statement. It tells you what happened to your investment. Your results can be different from the fund's overall results, especially if you enter or exit the fund during the fund's financial year. An informative account statement ought to contain the following information.

- The number of units that you held at the beginning and the end of the reporting period, including any purchases or redemptions.
- The value of a unit at the beginning and the end of the reporting period.
- The dollar value of your holding at the beginning and end of the reporting period.
- Details of investment returns, including the returns from capital gains and the returns from income.
- A comparison of the fund's performance relative to its benchmark.
- The dollar value of all fees and charges levied against your account.

You may not get an account statement containing this much detail. Some funds are notoriously lacking at disclosing details about performance and fees. If you want this type of disclosure, ask to see a sample account statement before you invest your money.

Fund reports

Reports to members are another source of performance information. Members' reports should include the following information.

- General commentary on the financial markets.
- Performance data for the fund together with an analysis of the portfolio's performance against its benchmark.
- The manager's outlook and strategy for the next period.
- Details about the assets held, their valuation, income received, distributions paid and the costs of managing the fund.
- Financial statements.

Fund managers use the Internet to distribute general information about the funds they manage. Their websites generally provide prices that are updated daily, a history of past performance, electronic downloading for Product Disclosure Statements and other forms, and information about the composition of each fund's portfolio. Here are some examples of fund manager websites.

- Hyperion Asset Management at *hyperion.com.au*
- Katana Asset Management at *katanaasset.com*
- Prime Value Asset Management at *primevalue.com.au*
- PM Capital at *pmcapital.com.au*
- First Sentier Investors at *firstsentierinvestors.com.au*
- Ausbil Investment Management at *ausbil.co.au*
- Bennelong Funds Management at *bennelongfunds.com*
- Platypus Asset Management at *platypusassetmanagement.com.au*

Research Organisations

There are research organisations that analyse the practices and performance of managed investments in Australia. Financial planners use this information to select funds that meet the risk profiles of their clients. Individual investors can use the same information to decide for themselves.

If you want to sift through the countless Australian managed investments that are on the market, these organisations are in the business of making the task easier. However, there is always some controversy about which organisation has the best methodology and the most reliable ratings. Here are some examples.

- Morningstar Research at *morningstar.com.au* provides comprehensive information for ETFs, LICs and unlisted funds in Australia and New Zealand. It is also known for its 'star' rating system. You can monitor how funds have been performing at *morningstar.com.au/tools/fund-screener.*

- Canstar at *canstar.com.au* covers the managed funds of forty Australian fund managers to help you compare hundreds of ETFs and managed funds. Canstar releases annual 'star' ratings for different categories of managed funds.

- Chant West at *chantwest.com.au* researches Australian superannuation funds and presents key information through their AppleCheck comparison tool.

- The APRA MySuper Heatmap at *apra.gov.au/super-annuation-heatmaps* uses a colour scheme to provide information about MySuper products for investment returns, fees and costs, and sustainability of member outcomes.

- SelectingSuper at *selectingsuper.com.au* provides superannuation fund performance tables researched by Rainmaker Information. They also have an annual publication called The Good Super Guide.

- The ATO website has a tool that can be used to compare the MySuper option across superannuation funds. It is called YourSuper Comparison Tool at *ato.gov.au/ calculators-and-tools/YourSuper-comparison-tool*.

The investment management industry is sensitive about performance figures that include the effects of fees. They prefer to quote gross performance figures that do not include deductions for fees. Gross performance figures reflect the investment performance of the fund, but they overstate the actual returns to individual investors.

RISK AND RETURN IN MANAGED INVESTMENTS

The *Sharpe Index* is one of the recognised ways to measure fund performance on a risk-adjusted basis. It is the average return above the risk-free rate of return adjusted for risk.

$$\text{Sharpe Index} = \frac{\text{Average fund rate of return} - \text{Average risk free rate of return}}{\text{Standard deviation of fund returns}}$$

The average fund rate of return is the average of the annual returns over a given period. The average risk-free rate of return is the average return from government bonds over the same period. The difference represents the returns associated with higher risk. Risk is measured statistically by the *standard deviation* of annual returns. A low standard deviation means that annual returns stay close to the average representing lower risk, and a high standard deviation means that annual returns are widely scattered representing higher risk. The Sharpe Index is a measure of a fund's risk-return tradeoff.

Unfortunately, Sharpe Index numbers are not easy to find because funds do not routinely disclose them. Sometimes they are published with fund performance information. The index numbers are not an absolute measure, what matters is the way they are used to rank funds' risk-return performance. The fund that is ranked best has the best combination of maximising rate of return and minimising risk, but it may not be the fund with the highest returns. For example, assume we have five funds with the following characteristics together with the benchmark index. The risk-free rate is 5 percent.

	Rate of Return	Standard Deviation	Sharpe Index
Fund A	18%	35%	.371
Fund B	18%	30%	.433
Fund C	16%	30%	.367
Fund D	16%	20%	.550
Fund E	14%	10%	.900
Benchmark index	**15%**	**20%**	**.500**

This is what the Sharpe Index tells us about the relative risk-return rankings. Funds A and B have the same rate of return, but Fund B has less risk. Therefore, Fund B has a higher Sharpe index than Fund A. Funds B and C have the same degree of risk, but Fund B has a greater rate of return. Therefore, Fund B has a higher Sharpe Index than Fund C. Four of the five funds outperformed the benchmark, however, three of them did it by taking more risk than the benchmark. Fund D outperformed the benchmark on the same degree of risk. The top ranked fund, however, is fund E. Even though it has the lowest rate of return, it has the best risk-return tradeoff and consequently the highest Sharpe Index.

AUSTRALIA SCORECARD

S&P Dow Jones Indices is a research organisation at *spglobal.com* that publish the 'SPIVA Australia Scorecard' in which they report the performance of actively managed funds against their benchmark indices. Funds are grouped into Australian shares, Australian small-cap and mid-cap shares, Australian funds that invest in international shares, Australian bonds, and Australian real estate investment trusts. They are based on net returns after fees have been deducted. For each group the percentage of funds that have not performed as well as their respective index is reported for the past 1, 3, 5, 10 and 15-year periods. Figure 8.2 is based on the SPIVA Australia Scorecard for actively managed Australian funds at 30 June 2021.

Figure 8.2 Percentage of underperforming active Australian funds

Fund Category	1 year	3 years	5 years	10 years	15 years
Shares	44.3	75.9	75.7	80.8	85.8
Small and mid-cap shares	35.0	49.6	65.3	55.1	50.0
International shares	54.6	78.1	81.9	90.6	94.8
Bonds	29.9	67.2	70.2	85.5	83.1
Real Estate	58.5	56.7	56.5	78.8	78.8

Comparing actively managed funds against their benchmark index is standard practice. Another test is how well past performance extends into the future. According to the SPIVA Report, out of the 234 Australian funds that beat their respective benchmark for the five-year period to June 2016 only 80 continued to outperform their benchmark during the following five-year period to June 2021.

The SPIVA Australia Scorecard suggests that the majority of fund managers find superior results difficult to achieve in both the short-term and the long-term. Superior performance depends on asset selection and investment timing. Most fund managers do a credible job of asset selection. Not even the best fund managers, however, are consistently superior at forecasting major turning points in the stockmarket. Nevertheless, the data also demonstrates there are some funds that do consistently perform better than their benchmark and reinforces the importance of being highly selective about the fund you choose.

One reason for poor performance is fees. If a fund manager succeeds in matching the benchmark, fees drag the net return below the benchmark and the fund appears to be underperforming. The irony is that to match the benchmark, a fund manager needs to outperform it enough to cover fees. Even a passive index fund that perfectly matches the returns from its index would appear to be underperforming to the extent that fees are deducted from investment returns.

Another reason why so many fund managers turn in a poor performance is because it is in their interest to play it safe. If a manager's performance falls behind the benchmark, then investors will leave the fund and invest elsewhere. If the manager tries to beat the benchmark, they run a greater risk that they may fail. So they invest cautiously in a selection of securities that does not stray too far from the benchmark profile. It is known in the industry that many 'active' managers are more conservative than they claim to be.

SUMMARY

If you choose to invest in a managed fund, you need to consider whether you want one that is passively managed or actively managed. Knowing the potential advantages and disadvantages of each approach will help you determine which best matches your investment objectives. Compared with direct investing, managed investments incur additional costs. Fee structures vary between ETFs, LICs, unlisted funds, and superannuation funds. Management fees are payable no matter how well a fund performs. Investors in managed funds have several sources of information about the performance of managed investments including account statements, fund reports, and research organisation websites. The Sharpe Index is a method for ranking managed funds according to their risk/return tradeoff. The evidence suggests that active fund managers in Australia find consistent superior performance difficult to achieve.

Part D

OPTIONS AND FUTURES

Options and futures contracts are financial instruments that represent a claim on another asset. The value of an option or futures contract is directly linked to the value of the underlying asset. They are a legitimate investment medium that may appeal to more aggressive investors, and they can also be used to hedge against risk for more conservative investors. They are complex instruments, however, that need to be fully understood before taking the plunge. As a result, they are not recommended until an investor has gained considerable experience in the stockmarket. Part D explains the features and investment strategies for exchange traded options and financial futures.

CHAPTER **9**

EXCHANGE TRADED
OPTIONS

Most of the trading in exchange traded options (ETOs) consists
of put and call options on a selected number of listed Australian
shares. However, ETOs also include low exercise price options
(LEPOs), warrants, and index options. The purpose of this
chapter is to examine the nature of exchange traded options and
how they operate as an investment medium.

SHARE OPTIONS

Option contracts on the shares of over 70 Australian companies
trade on the ASX. You buy and sell them through your
stockbroker just as you would buy and sell shares. These option
contracts are standardised, which means that they conform to a
set of specifications that are prescribed by the Exchange. A share
option conveys to its buyer, or *holder*, the right, but not the
obligation, to trade in the underlying shares at a specified price
on or before the expiry date. This right is granted by the seller, or
writer, of the option. A *call option* conveys the right to purchase
100 underlying shares. If you exercise a call, the writer is obliged
to sell them to you at the exercise price. A *put option* conveys
the right to sell 100 underlying shares. If you exercise a put, the
writer is obliged to buy them from you at the exercise price.

Exercise price

The *exercise price*, also called the *strike price*, is the share price at which an option can be exercised. Exercise prices are set at intervals above and below the current market price of the underlying share. As the share price moves, new exercise prices become available so that more volatile shares will have options with a greater range of exercise prices. There are matching puts and calls for every exercise price.

If the current market price of the underlying share is greater than the exercise price, then a call option is said to be *in-the-money* because the holder can buy the underlying shares for less than the market price. If the market price of the underlying share is less than the exercise price, then a call option is *out-of-the-money*. The opposite conditions apply to put options. If the exercise price is equal to the market price of the underlying shares, an option is *at-the-money*.

	Call Option	Put Option
Share Price > Exercise Price	In-the-money	Out-of-the-money
Share Price < Exercise Price	Out-of-the-money	In-the-money
Share Price = Exercise Price	At-the-money	At-the-money

Expiry date

The *expiry date* occurs on the Thursday before the last Friday of a contract month. The option holder must decide by the expiry date whether to resell the option, exercise it, or allow it to lapse. ASX equity options are *American-style* options which means they can be exercised at any time up to and including the expiry date. A *European-style* option can only be exercised on the expiry date. Options begin trading about nine months before the expiry date and three contract months usually trade simultaneously.

Adjustments

The exercise price and/or the number of underlying shares will be adjusted to reflect the effects of any bonus issues, cash issues, consolidations or capital reconstructions. The idea is that an option holder should not be disadvantaged when changes occur to the capital structure of the company. No adjustment is made, however, as a result of the declaration of a dividend. Cash dividends paid on the underlying shares affect the option premium through the ex-dividend effect on the share price. Since the share price is expected to fall by the amount of the cash dividend, it implies a lower call price and a higher put price.

Premium

The price paid for an option is called the *premium*. It should not be confused with the exercise price or the price of the underlying shares. Option premiums are quoted on a per share basis. The option premium is the only part of an option contract that is not standardised. It is determined by buyers and sellers trading on the ASX. There are six elements that are responsible for determining the premium for a share option. They can be divided into intrinsic value and time value.

Only in-the-money options have *intrinsic value*. The intrinsic value of an in-the-money call option is the difference between the price of the underlying shares and the exercise price. The intrinsic value of a put option is the difference between the exercise price and the price of the underlying shares. The greater the intrinsic value, the greater the option premium.

All options have *time value* until they expire. For in-the-money options, time value is the difference between the option premium and its intrinsic value. Out-of-the-money options consist only of time value. Options are frequently described as a wasting asset because they lose time value as they approach expiry. An option will lose about one-third of its time value during the first half of its life and two-thirds of its time value during the second half of its life.

- The more time remaining until expiry, the greater the time value and hence the higher the option premium. The reason is because there is more time for the underlying share price to move into a position that makes the option profitable.

- The more volatile the underlying share price, the greater the time value and hence the higher the option premium. The reason is because greater volatility increases the possibility that the underlying share price will fluctuate into a profitable position.

- Higher interest rates generally result in higher call option premiums and lower put option premiums. The reason is that the rate of interest represents the carrying cost for controlling the underlying shares.

- When the underlying shares go ex-dividend, the share price will fall by the amount of the dividend. A call option premium will fall, and a put option premium will rise proportionally to the size of the dividend.

The elements that drive the option premium are tied together mathematically by the Black-Scholes Option Pricing Model. Its purpose is to establish a fair value for a call option premium. Different versions of the model are used for a variety of option contracts. It is a rather daunting equation that does not easily lend itself to manual calculation. Fortunately, there are websites that do the calculations for you.

Closing out

There is more than one way to terminate or *close out* an option position. It is not always necessary to exercise an option in order to realise a gain or loss. Option gains or losses can be realised at any time before expiration by making a closing transaction consisting of reselling a bought option or buying back a sold option. To exercise an option, the purchase or sale of the underlying shares takes place at the exercise price. If an option is out-of-the-money at expiration, it automatically expires worthless. If an option is in-the-money at expiration, it is usually closed out by your stockbroker.

BUYING A CALL

Buying a call is a strategy designed to benefit from an increase in the price of the underlying shares. The potential loss is limited to the amount paid for the call premium. The potential gains, however, are virtually unlimited. Figure 9.1 is the profit profile for buying a call. The vertical axis represents the gain or loss on the call option premium and the horizontal axis represents the corresponding price of the underlying shares. In this example, the call begins at-the-money in which both the current price of the underlying shares and the exercise price is $2.00. The call option premium is 5 cents per share. The amount of the call premium is the maximum potential loss if the price of the underlying shares falls below the exercise price. It will break even if the price of the underlying share rises above the exercise price by the amount of the premium to $2.05. The potential profit is unlimited and depends on the extent to which the price of the underlying shares rise above the breakeven point. Leverage is one of the big attractions for buying options. Consider the difference between investing in shares at a market price of $2.00 or buying a call on the same shares with an exercise price of $2.00 for a premium of 5 cents per share. If the share price increases by $1.00 to $3.00, the return on an investment in the shares is 50 percent. At the same time, the call premium will also increase by $1.00 resulting in an increase on the call premium of 2000 percent.

Figure 9.1 Buying a call

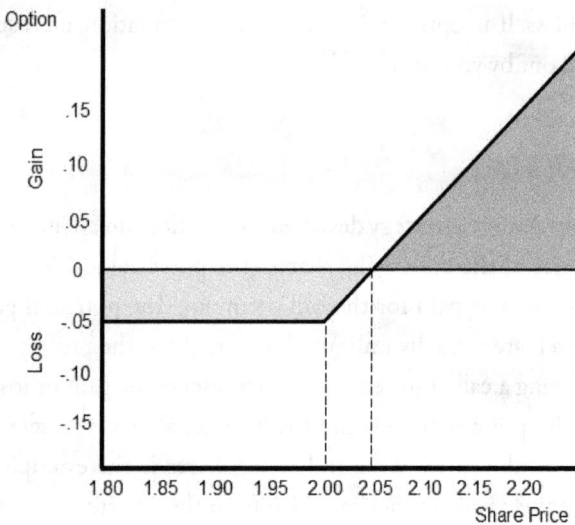

Some investors buy calls as part of an overall investment plan. A popular strategy consists of placing 10 percent of their funds into calls on selected shares and the other 90 percent into low-risk fixed income securities. This strategy enables them to benefit from an increase in share prices while limiting downside risk to the call premium. Other investors use calls to lock in a purchase price until they have sufficient cash available to pay for the shares.

BUYING A PUT

Buying a put is a strategy designed to benefit from a fall in the price of the underlying shares. The potential loss is limited to the amount paid for the put premium. The potential reward depends on how far the underlying share price falls. Put options provide a more attractive method than short selling because they not only offer greater leverage, but also a known and predetermined risk. Figure 9.2 represents the profit profile for buying a put.

Figure 9.2 Buying a put

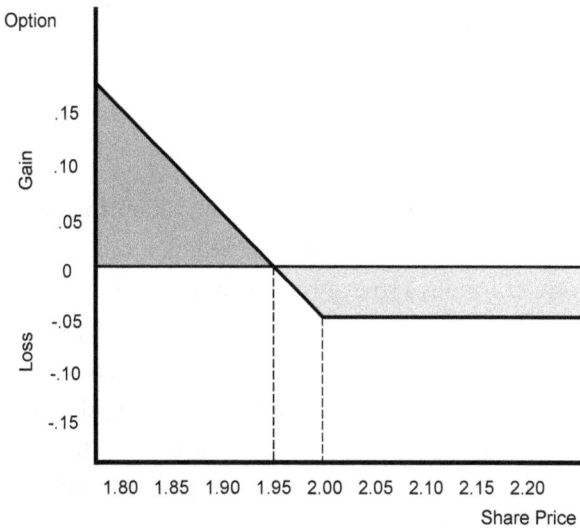

In this example, the put begins at-the-money in which both the current price of the underlying share and the exercise price is $2.00. The put option premium is 5 cents per share. The amount of the put premium is the maximum potential loss if the price of the underlying shares remains greater than the exercise price until expiry. The breakeven point will be reached if the price of the underlying shares falls below the exercise price by the amount of the premium. The potential profit depends on the extent to which the price of the underlying shares falls below the breakeven point.

Some investors limit the risk of owning shares by simultaneously buying a put over them. This strategy limits their risk by establishing a minimum selling price for the shares and yields a profit to the extent that the share price increases by more than the put premium. The same strategy can be used to protect unrealised profits.

SELLING A CALL

Selling share options is a high risk proposition that is mostly dominated by financial institutions. Selling a call is known as writing a call and is a strategy designed to benefit from a fall in the price of the underlying share. A call seller is obligated to sell the underlying shares at the exercise price if they are assigned an exercise notice to do so. For assuming this obligation, the call seller receives the call premium. A call seller holds the opposite view to a call buyer. Figure 9.3 is the profit profile for selling a call.

Figure 9.3 Selling a Call

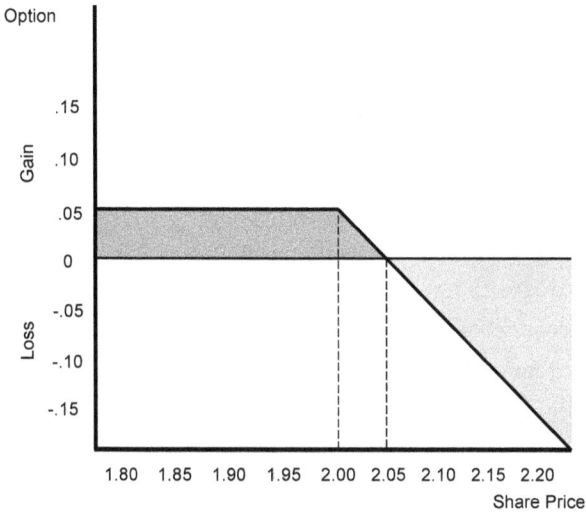

In this example, the call begins at-the-money in which both the current price of the underlying shares and the exercise price is $2.00. The call option premium is 5 cents per share. The amount of the call premium is the maximum potential profit if the price of the underlying shares remains below the exercise price until expiry. The trade will break even if the price of the underlying shares rises above the exercise price by the amount of the premium to $2.05. Potential losses are virtually unlimited and depend on the extent to which the price of the underlying shares rise above the breakeven point.

The risks involved in selling a call depend on whether the call is *covered*. A covered call writing strategy consists of selling a call on underlying shares that are already owned. It enables the seller to earn income equal to the call premium resulting in either additional returns or a cushion against a price decline in the underlying shares. If the underlying share price increases substantially, however, the holder will call them away at the exercise price. Selling at-the-money or in-the-money calls generates higher premium income, but it also gives up a larger proportion of the upside potential in the share price. Selling out-of-the-money calls generates less premium income, but it retains some participation in any rise in the share price.

Covered call writing is a more conservative strategy compared with uncovered call writing. The objective of selling an uncovered call is also to realise premium income but without owning the underlying shares. Uncovered options are sometimes called 'naked' options. An uncovered call writer must deposit and maintain sufficient margin with their stockbroker to ensure that they can acquire the underlying shares if the call is exercised. The risk is like short selling except that it is cushioned by the premium income.

SELLING A PUT

Selling a put, also called writing a put, is perhaps the least understood of the four basic option strategies. Selling a put is a strategy designed to benefit from an increase in the price of the underlying shares. A put writer is obligated to buy the underlying shares at the exercise price if they are assigned an exercise notice to do so. For assuming this obligation, they receive the put premium. A put seller holds the opposite view to the put buyer about the likely future price of the underlying asset. Figure 9.4 is the profit profile for selling a put.

In this example, the put begins at-the-money in which both the current price of the underlying shares and the exercise price is

$2.00. The put option premium is 5 cents per share. The amount of the put premium is the maximum potential profit if the price of the underlying shares remains above the exercise price until expiry. It will break even if the price of the underlying shares falls below the exercise price by the amount of the premium to $1.95. Potential losses are virtually unlimited and depend on the extent to which the price of the underlying shares falls below the breakeven point.

Figure 9.4 Selling a put

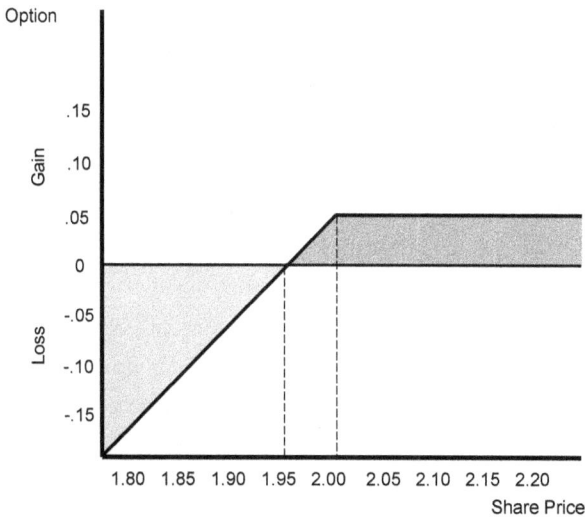

The risks involved in selling puts depend on whether the put is covered. A covered put writing strategy consists of having a corresponding short position in the underlying shares. An uncovered seller does not have a corresponding short position in the shares so they must deposit sufficient margin with their stockbroker.

8

COMBINATIONS

You can buy and sell combinations of options to achieve a particular position relative to the underlying shares. For example, suppose you think the underlying share price is going to move substantially but you are not sure if it will be up or down. You can buy a *straddle* consisting of a call option and a put option at the same exercise price and expiry date. Whichever way the underlying share price moves, you will profit if the price moves by more than the combined option premiums.

A *strap* is a bullish strategy that consists of two at-the-money call options and one at-the-money put option with the same expiration date. If the share price goes up enough to cover the combined option premiums, the first call is exercised and the holder can ride the remaining straddle for free. If the share price goes down, the put can be exercised to recover some or all of the combined option premiums.

A *strip* is a bearish strategy that consists of two at-the-money put options and one at-the-money call option with the same expiration date. If the share price goes down enough to cover the combined option premiums, the first put is exercised and the holder can ride the remaining straddle for free. If the share price goes up, the call can be exercised to recover some or all of the combined option premiums.

LOW EXERCISE PRICE OPTIONS

Low exercise price options, or LEPOs, are extremely deep-in-the-money call options. A LEPO covers 100 shares and has an exercise price of one cent per share. These are European-style options that may only be exercised at expiry, but they can be bought and sold at any time prior to expiry. Inasmuch as LEPOs are extremely deep-in-the-money, the premium moves in tandem with the price of the underlying shares. Unlike conventional share options, the LEPO premium is not paid in full but can be margined so they are also highly leveraged. LEPOs are traded on more than 100 listed companies and the S&P/ASX 200 Index. The nature of a LEPO means that it has just about the same risk profile as an equivalent futures contract.

WARRANTS

A warrant is essentially a long-dated option that is issued by a third party and traded on the ASX or the Chi-X. Warrants are not a contract created by the exchange, nor are they guaranteed by the exchange. They are generally issued by large financial institutions which means that the warrant holder is exposed to the financial and business risks associated with the warrant issuer.

Warrants are not standardised contracts so the terms of issue may vary considerably from one warrant to another. They may be written over individual shares, a portfolio of shares, indices, currencies, fixed income securities or commodities. They may be American-style or European-style and delivery may be settled in cash or the underlying securities. Warrants do not have to be exercised to realise a profit if they can be resold, however market liquidity for some warrants is thin.

The warrant premium is affected by several factors in common with other types of options. These include the current price and price volatility of the underlying asset, the level of interest rates, the exercise price, and the time to expiry. Since they are essentially long-dated options, warrants are more expensive than standard share options because of the time value component. Warrant premiums may also be affected by other factors including the credit risk of the issuer, extraordinary events affecting the terms of issue, possible illiquidity in the secondary market, and potential adjustments resulting from a bonus share issue, a rights issue, or a dividend payment. The Product Disclosure Statement, sometimes called the 'Offering Circular', contains the specifications for a warrant and how it is structured.

Call equity warrants and put equity warrants are issued over the shares of listed companies. They are the most common type of warrant traded. The exercise price is usually close to the share price at the time of issue. They can be American-style or European-style and the expiry date generally varies from six months to three years. If they are exercised, settlement may be in cash or delivery of the underlying shares.

An issuer is not necessarily obliged to hold the underlying shares in order to issue the warrants. Fully covered warrants means the issuer has placed the underlying shares into a trust or similar arrangement in order to guarantee delivery if the warrant holder chooses to exercise. The purpose of fully covered warrants is to reduce any issuer risk to the warrant holder.

INDEX OPTIONS

Index options are standardised puts and calls on the S&P/ASX 200 Index. They can be used to hedge or speculate on broad movements in the Australian stockmarket. If you expect the stockmarket to go up, you could go long by buying a call. If you expect the stockmarket to go down, you could go short by buying a put. Each index point is equal to $10. The option premiums are quoted as index points with exercise intervals every 25 index points. For example, if you buy an index option with a premium of 50 points, you will pay $500 plus brokerage fees. Contract months are March, June, September and December These are European-style options that are only exercisable on the day of expiry, but they can be bought and sold at any time prior to expiry. You receive a cash payment on exercising an in-the-money index option.

SUMMARY

Exchange Traded Options (ETOs) mainly consist of put and call options on a selected number of listed shares, however ETOs also include low exercise price options (LEPOs), warrants, and index options. You can buy and sell them through your stockbroker just as you would buy and sell shares. A call option conveys the right to purchase the underlying asset at the exercise price up until the expiry date. A put option conveys the right to sell the underlying asset at the exercise price up until the expiry date. The price of an option is called the premium and it is determined by buyers and sellers. Low exercise price options have an exercise price of one cent per share and the premium moves in tandem with the share price. Warrants are long dated options that are generally issued by large financial institutions. Index options are used to hedge or speculate on broad movements in the stockmarket.

CHAPTER 10

FINANCIAL FUTURES

A futures contract is a legally binding agreement to buy or sell a standard quantity of an underlying asset on a future date for a price agreed upon today. There are futures contracts for commodities such as wool, wheat, oil, gold and electricity, and there are futures contracts for financial instruments such as a stockmarket indices or fixed income securities.

Futures contracts were developed as a risk management tool to hedge against price volatility in the underlying assets. For hedging buyers, futures contracts provide a means for locking in the price today at which they will buy the underlying asset in the future. Hedging sellers use futures contracts to lock in the price now that they will receive for selling the underlying asset in the future. However, futures contracts are also a highly leveraged vehicle for traders who want to speculate on price movements in the underlying assets. The purpose of this chapter is to explore the financial futures contracts that trade on the ASX.

TRADING IN FUTURES

Not all brokers offer futures trading. When a futures broker opens your account, they will provide you with a Product Disclosure Statement. Read it carefully and make sure you understand how futures contracts operate and the obligations of those who enter into them. You will be asked to acknowledge the risks in futures trading in a client agreement setting out the contractual terms upon which you and the broker will deal. You will also need to deposit sufficient funds into your account before you can place an order.

Participants in the futures market consist of hedgers and speculators. Hedgers seek to reduce the risk of price volatility from holding a position in the underlying asset by taking the opposite position in a futures contract. For example, hedge transactions can be used to protect against changes in interest rates or changes in a stockmarket index. Large companies, banks, life insurance companies and similar organisations face huge risks if interest rates or share prices change unexpectedly. They use futures contracts to hedge against unexpected changes and thereby protect themselves against these risks.

Speculators accept the risk of price volatility in an attempt to profit from correctly anticipating movements in interest rates or share prices. Although their role is often misunderstood, speculators are essential for the efficient operation of a futures market because their willingness to assume risk provides the means for hedgers to transfer it. Speculation in futures contracts can be highly profitable. It is also very risky, and speculators should only risk money they can afford to lose.

When you buy or sell a futures contract, you are trading the obligation to take delivery (if you are the buyer) or to make delivery (if you are the seller) of the underlying asset at a specific time in the future for a price that was agreed when the trade took place. However, futures contracts are rarely delivered because they are closed out by the purchase or sale of equal and opposite contracts. Moreover, most of the underlying financial instruments are notional, which means that they do not actually exist and delivery can only be made in cash.

The price of a futures contract normally differs from the price of the underlying asset which is known as the 'spot price'. The longer the time to maturity, the greater will be the futures price relative to the spot price. Increases/decreases in interest rates will cause the futures price to increase/decrease relative to the spot price. Actual futures prices, however, do not always behave in precisely this way because they also reflect expectations about future movements in the spot price.

Financial futures consist of index futures and interest rate futures. The leading index contracts are ASX SPI 200 Index futures, Mini ASX SPI 200 Index futures, and ASX 200 A-REIT Index futures. The leading interest rate contracts are ninety day bank bill futures, three-year bond futures, five-year bond futures, ten-year bond futures and twenty-year bond futures. These correspond to various points on the yield curve. A futures contract is standardised in all respects except for the price which is determined in the market between buyers and sellers. The following terms are uniform in a futures contract.

- **Contract unit** - The quantity of the underlying asset covered by one contract.
- **Delivery** - The quality of the underlying asset which may be delivered. Financial futures are generally delivered for an equivalent amount in cash.
- **Quotation** - The way in which the contract price will be quoted including the minimum fluctuation.
- **Contract Months** - The month in which a contract becomes deliverable. Futures contracts generally trade in several different contract months.
- **Expiry** - The day on which trading terminates.

An opening position in a futures contract may be either bought (going *long* in anticipation of a rise in the futures price) or sold (going *short* in anticipation of a fall in the futures price). To *close out* a futures position you trade in the opposite direction. If you are long in a futures contract, you sell a contract to close out your position, and if you are short in a futures contract, you buy a contract to close out your position. You do not need to worry about who you bought from or sold to because the ASX acts as the counterparty on all contracts.

You are required to put up a deposit for each new contract position known as the *initial margin*. The amount of the initial margin is determined by the ASX Clearing House, and it depends on the price volatility of the underlying asset. It provides the Clearing House with security to cover the credit risk of a party defaulting on a contact. The initial margin is repaid when the contract position is closed out.

In addition to the initial margin, there is *variation margin* which reflects movements in the futures price. You are required to pay variation margin whenever the futures price moves against you. Failure to meet a margin call will automatically result in your position being closed out by your broker. You receive a variation margin credit whenever the futures price moves in your favour. This process is called *mark to market* and its purpose is to maintain the balance of the initial margin.

Futures trading provides leveraged exposure to moves in the underlying asset. The initial margin is usually in the range of 5 to 10 percent of the value of the futures contract. If the market moves in your favour, the return on the futures contract will be many times greater than the movement in the underlying asset. However, leveraged exposure can also lead to substantial losses. If the market moves against you, the losses in the futures contract will be many times greater than the movement in the underlying asset. It is important to decide if this kind of risk is appropriate in your circumstances.

Let's say you buy a futures contract at $50,000 and the initial margin is $2,500. Later, you close out (sell) when the contract price reaches $55,000. The increase in the price of the contract is 10 percent, but the profit from your trade is $5,000 or 200 percent on your initial margin of $2,500. If the price falls to $45,000, your broker will ask for $5,000 in variation margin to maintain the balance of the initial margin. The decrease in the price of the contract is 10 percent. The loss from your trade is $5,000 or 200 percent on your initial margin of $2,500.

INDEX FUTURES

Index futures have a few advantages over a portfolio of shares. Liquidity is generally better, brokerage costs are lower, and it is easier to go short with futures than it is with shares. Only one order is required, the cash required is lower, and there is greater leverage with margin trading. Most of the trading in index futures is in ASX SPI 200 futures, Mini ASX SPI 200 futures, and ASX 200 A-REIT futures.

ASX SPI 200 Futures

The ASX SPI 200 Index futures contract enables traders to hedge against or speculate on broad movements in the Australian stockmarket. The S&P/ASX 200 Index represents approximately 80 percent of the capitalisation of listed shares in Australia. Since the S&P/ASX 200 Index does not physically exist, ASX SPI 200 futures contracts are settled with an equivalent sum in cash. A trader anticipating a rise in the stockmarket will go long ASX SPI 200 futures, whereas a trader anticipating a decline in the stockmarket will go short ASX SPI 200 futures. The ASX SPI 200 futures contract consists of the following terms.

- **Contract Unit** - A sum of money equal to twenty-five times the S&P/ASX 200 Share Price Index, equivalent to $175,000 at 7000 index points.
- **Delivery** - Cash only.
- **Quotation** - In the same form as the S&P/ASX 200. The minimum fluctuation is one index point and is equal to $25.00.
- **Contract Months** - March, June, September and December up to six quarter months ahead and the nearest two non-quarterly expiry months.
- **Expiry** - Last business day of the contract month.

There is also a related contract based on the S&P/ASX 200 Gross Total Return Index. It is identical to the S&P/ASX 200 contract except that it accounts for the reinvestment of dividends thus enabling traders to replicate the total return from a diversified portfolio of shares.

Mini ASX SPI 200 futures

Instead of trading the larger ASX SPI 200 futures contract, you can trade the smaller Mini ASX SPI 200 futures contract. The Mini ASX SPI 200 futures contract consists of the following terms.

- **Contract Unit** - A sum of money equal to five times the S&P/ASX 200 Share Price Index, equivalent to $35,000 at 7000 index points.
- **Delivery** - Cash only.

- **Quotation** - In the same form as the S&P/ASX 200. The minimum fluctuation is one index point and is equal to $5.00.

- **Contract Months** - March, June, September and December up to two quarter months ahead and the nearest two non-quarterly expiry months.

- **Expiry** - Last business day of the contract month.

ASX 200 A-REIT futures

The S&P/ASX 200 A-REIT Index consists of listed Australian Real Estate Investment Trusts (A-REITs) that own property such as shopping malls, hotels and office towers and derive income from rental returns.

- **Contract Unit** - A sum of money equal to twenty-five times the S&P/ASX 200 A-REIT Index, equivalent to $37,500 at 1500 index points.

- **Delivery** - Cash only.

- **Quotation** - In the same form as the S&P/ASX 200 A-REIT Index. The minimum fluctuation is one index point and is equal to $25.00.

- **Contract Months** - March, June, September and December up to four quarters ahead.

- **Expiry** - Last business day of the contract month.

INTEREST RATE FUTURES

Interest rate futures can be used to either hedge or speculate on changes in interest rates. Like bonds, the price of interest rate futures varies inversely with market interest rates. Higher interest rates will lower the price of interest rate futures and lower interest rates will increase the price of interest rate futures. Interest rate futures include Ninety-day bank accepted bill futures and three-year, five-year, ten-year, and twenty-year bond futures. These contracts correspond to different points on the yield curve.

Ninety-day bank bill futures

Bank accepted bills of exchange (bank bills) are negotiable fixed income securities that are sold at a discount for periods that are generally between 30 and 180 days. A bank bill represents a promise to pay the full face value on maturity and it is backed by the credit rating of the bank that has accepted or guaranteed its repayment.

Ninety-day bank bill futures provide traders with the means to take a position in anticipation of fluctuations in short-term interest rates. The bank bill contract represents an agreement to borrow or lend money for ninety days from a future date at an interest rate agreed upon today. The ninety-day bank bill futures contract consists of the following terms.

- **Contract Unit** - $1,000,000 face value of ninety-day bank accepted bills of exchange whose term to maturity will begin on the settlement day.

- **Delivery** - Bank accepted bills of exchange or negotiable certificates of deposit or their equivalent maturing 85-95 days from settlement.

- **Quotation** - 100.00 percent minus the annual percent yield in multiples of 0.01 percent. The minimum fluctuation of 0.01 percent, or one *tick*, is approximately $24 but varies with the level of interest rates. Here are examples of the quote, the implied annual yield, and the corresponding dollar value of a contract.

Quote	Implied Yield %	$ Value
100.00	0.00	1,000,000.00
95.00	5.00	987,821.38
90.00	10.00	975,935.82

- **Contract Months** - March, June, September and December up to five years ahead.
- **Expiry** - The second Friday of the contract month.

If short term interest rates rise, then the value of bank bills will fall. Conversely, if short term interest rates decline, then the value of bank bills will increase. If a trader is anticipating a rise in 90-day bank bill interest rates they will go short (sell) bank bill futures. On the other hand, if they think there will be a decline in 90-day bank bill interest rates they will go long (buy) bank bill futures.

Three-year bond futures

Three-year bond futures contracts provide traders with the means to hedge against or speculate on fluctuations in medium-term interest rates. The three year bond futures contract consists of the following terms.

- **Contract Unit** - A notional Commonwealth Government Treasury Bond with a face value of $100,000, a coupon rate of 6 percent per annum and a term to maturity of three years.
- **Delivery** - Cash only.
- **Quotation** - 100.00 percent minus the annual percent yield in multiples of 0.005 percent. The minimum fluctuation of 0.005 percent equals approximately $15.00 per tick but varies with the level of interest rates.

- **Contract Months** - March, June, September and December up to two quarters ahead.
- **Expiry** - The 15th day of the contract month.

If medium-term interest rates rise, then the value of three-year bonds will fall. Similarly, if medium-term interest rates fall, then the value of three-year bonds will rise. Therefore, a trader anticipating a rise in medium-term interest rates will go short three-year bond futures, whereas a trader anticipating a decline in medium-term interest rates will go long three-year bond futures.

Five-year bond futures

Five-year bond futures contracts provide traders with the means to hedge against or speculate on fluctuations in intermediate-term interest rates. The five-year bond futures contract consists of the following terms.

- **Contract Unit** - A notional Commonwealth Government Treasury Bond with a face value of $100,000, a coupon rate of 2 percent per annum and a term to maturity of five years.
- **Delivery** - Cash only.
- **Quotation** - 100.00 percent minus the annual percent yield in multiples of 0.005 percent. The minimum fluctuation of 0.005 percent equals approximately $26.00 per tick but varies with the level of interest rates.
- **Contract Months** - March, June, September and December up to two quarters ahead.
- **Expiry** - The 15th day of the contract month.

If intermediate-term interest rates rise, then the value of five-year bonds will fall. Similarly, if intermediate-term interest rates fall, then the value of five-year bonds will rise. Therefore, a trader anticipating a rise in medium-term interest rates will go short five-year bond futures, whereas a trader anticipating a decline in intermediate-term interest rates will go long five-year bond futures.

Ten-year bond futures
Ten-year bond futures provide traders with the means to hedge against or speculate on fluctuations in long-term interest rates. The ten-year bond futures contract consists of the following terms.

- **Contract Unit** - A notional Commonwealth Government Treasury Bond with a face value of $100,000, a coupon rate of 6 percent per annum and a term to maturity of ten years.
- **Delivery** - Cash only.
- **Quotation** - 100.00 percent minus the annual percent yield in multiples of 0.005 percent. The minimum fluctuation of 0.005 percent equals approximately $47.00 per tick but varies with the level of interest rates.
- **Contract Months** - March, June, September and December up to two quarters ahead.
- **Expiry** - The 15th day of the contract month.

If long-term interest rates rise, then the value of ten-year bonds will fall. Similarly, if long-term interest rates decline, then the value of ten-year bonds will increase. Therefore, a trader anticipating a rise in long-term interest rates will go short ten-year bond futures, whereas a trader anticipating a decline in long-term interest rates will go long ten-year bond futures.

Twenty-year bond futures

Twenty-year bond futures contracts provide traders with the means to hedge against or speculate on fluctuations in very long-term interest rates. The twenty-year bond futures contract consists of the following terms.

- **Contract Unit** - A notional Commonwealth Government Treasury Bond with a face value of $65,000, a coupon rate of 4 percent per annum and a term to maturity of twenty years.

- **Delivery** - Cash only.

- **Quotation** - 100.00 percent minus the annual percent yield in multiples of 0.005 percent. The minimum fluctuation of 0.005 percent equals approximately $50.00 per tick but varies with the level of interest rates.

- **Contract Months** - March, June, September and December up to two quarters ahead.

- **Expiry** - The 15th day of the contract month.

If very long-term interest rates rise, then the value of twenty-year bonds will fall. Similarly, if very long-term interest rates fall, then the value of twenty-year bonds will rise. Therefore, a trader anticipating a rise in very long-term interest rates will go short twenty-year bond futures, whereas a trader anticipating a decline in very long-term interest rates will go long twenty-year bond futures.

COMBINATIONS

There is a lot more to futures trading than simply taking a long or short contract position. Some futures traders prefer to base their trading strategy on the relationship between different futures contracts rather than taking an outright long or short position on individual contracts. A spread strategy consists of simultaneously taking a long position and a short position either in different contracts or different delivery months. In most cases, the minimum initial margin covering the two contracts is considerably less than the minimum initial margin on a single position.

If a spread is on different contracts, such as a three-year bond futures contract and a ten-year bond futures contract, it is called an 'inter-commodity spread'. An example is yield curve trading. If you expect the yield curve to shift from descending to ascending, then you would sell ten-year bond contracts and buy three-year bond contracts to profit from the change in their relative positions on the new yield curve.

A spread can also be on different delivery months in the same contract, such as a June ASX SPI 200 contract and a December ASX SPI 200 contract. A 'positive spread' is one in which the near month is bought and the distant month is sold. A 'negative spread' is the opposite in which the near month is sold and the distant month is bought. Deciding which contract to buy and which to sell depends on the current state of the market and how you expect it to change.

SUMMARY

Futures trading is not recommended for a first time investor. It may be something to keep in mind if you want to speculate after you have gained experience. A futures contract is a legally binding agreement to buy or sell a standard quantity of an underlying asset on a future date for a price agreed upon today.

Futures contracts were developed as a risk management tool to hedge against price volatility in the underlying assets. However, futures contracts are also a highly leveraged vehicle for traders who want to speculate on price movements in the underlying assets. Not all brokers offer futures trading. When a futures broker opens an account, they will provide a Product Disclosure Statement and a client agreement that acknowledges your obligations when you trade futures.

Financial futures consist of index futures and interest rate futures. The leading share index contracts are ASX SPI 200 Index futures, Mini ASX SPI 200 Index futures, and ASX 200 A-REIT Index futures. The leading interest rate contracts are ninety day bank bill futures, three-year bond futures, five-year bond futures, ten-year bond futures and twenty-year bond futures.

There is a lot more to futures trading than simply taking a long or short contract position. Some futures traders prefer to base their trading strategy on the relationship between different futures contracts rather than taking an outright long or short position on individual contracts.

Part **E**

INVESTING IN FIXED INCOME SECURITIES

Why do some investors buy fixed income securities when history tells us that higher rates of return have been earned from investing in shares? The answer lies in one's ability and willingness to accept risk. Shares are more volatile than fixed income securities and dividend payments are not fixed but paid at the discretion of a board of directors. Fixed income securities are not without risk either, but the risks are generally less than for shares. Facing less risk, investors in fixed income securities are generally prepared to accept lower returns.

For decades investing in fixed income securities was considered the least glamorous sector of the financial markets. In the 1980s fixed income securities experienced unprecedented price volatility because of tremendous swings in interest rates. This changed the nature of investing in fixed income securities from passive buy and hold strategies to more aggressive strategies that could produce considerable capital gains over relatively short periods. Fast forward to today, however, and investors in fixed income securities face a new challenge in the form of unprecedented low interest rates. Part E explains the features and investment strategies for fixed income securities.

CHAPTER 11

FEATURES OF FIXED INCOME SECURITIES

Fixed income securities are sometimes referred to as debt securities, interest rate securities, bonds, debentures, or notes. Investors in fixed income securities are lenders or creditors whereas share investors are part owners. A fixed income security has a limited life or maturity, whereas shares have a continuous life. Investors in fixed income securities receive interest payments in which the amount and timing are known in advance, whereas share investors generally receive dividends when and if they are declared.

Most fixed income securities are traded by dealers in the unlisted market. The dealers are financial institutions that trade with each other and with institutional investors. Access to the market for fixed income securities by private investors is limited because they do not normally invest the minimum amounts required by financial institutions. There are some fixed income securities, however, that private investors can buy and sell on the ASX through their stockbroker.

Fixed income securities are issued by the Commonwealth government, state governments, semi-government agencies and companies. There are different types of fixed income securities that vary in terms of the issuer, risk, return, marketability, maturity, and the frequency of interest payments. The purpose of this chapter is to consider the role of fixed income securities in investing, describe the main types of fixed income securities available to private investors, explain the nature of risk and return in fixed income securities, and examine how changes in market interest rates affect the returns from fixed income securities.

ROLE OF FIXED INCOME INVESTMENTS

Fixed income securities can provide an investor with regular cash flows, liquidity, low risk and diversification. These become increasingly important as an investor approaches retirement by increasing the stability of their income and reducing the level of risk. A high growth portfolio, which is typically suited for investors with significant years to retirement, is unlikely to have a significant allocation to fixed income securities, whereas a conservative portfolio for a retiree is likely to have a greater allocation to fixed income securities. Unfortunately, with interest rates at historic lows, some investors who relied on fixed income securities for their income have been forced into other types of investments with higher yields but at a greater risk.

The big investors in fixed income securities are the superannuation funds. Over one fifth of superannuation savings in Australia is invested in fixed income securities. If most of your retirement savings are in a superannuation fund, you already have exposure to fixed income securities and further investment as a private investor may not be warranted. If you are investing privately for your retirement, or you have a self-managed superannuation fund, you may want to consider fixed income securities as you get older.

The fixed income securities that are readily available to private investors are Exchange-traded Treasury bonds, listed company bonds and notes, and hybrid securities. There are basic features that apply to all types of fixed income securities.

- The amount of the loan is called its *par value* or *face value*.
- The interest rate is known as the *coupon rate*.
- The interest dates are when interest payments are made.
- The *maturity* date is when the issuer promises to repay the face value.
    - ◦ It is considered short term if there is less than one year to maturity.
    - ◦ It is considered medium term if there is one to three years to maturity.
    - ◦ It is considered long term if there is more than three years to maturity.
- The market price is determined by buyers and sellers, and it may be more or less than the face value.
- The *yield* is the rate of return on a fixed income security.
- *Basis points* refers to a common unit of measure for changes in yield. A 1 percent change in yield equals 100 basis points and a 0.01 percent change in yield equals 1 basis point.

EXCHANGE-TRADED COMMONWEALTH BONDS

Commonwealth government bonds are medium to long-term fixed income securities issued by the Treasury. Bonds issued by the Commonwealth government are AAA rated and they are the largest and most liquid segment of the market. In 2013 the Commonwealth government and the ASX introduced Exchange-traded Treasury Bonds and Exchange-traded Treasury

Indexed Bonds. This was done to enable private investors to gain access to government securities to diversify their investment portfolios.

Exchange-traded Treasury Bonds

Exchange-traded Treasury Bonds (eTBs) are a convenient and easily accessible way to invest in Australian Government Treasury Bonds. An eTB holder has beneficial ownership of Australian Government Treasury Bonds in the form of CHESS Depository Interests (CDIs) over which the eTBs have been issued. There is a range of eTBs available, and you will find them quoted on the ASX website. You can buy and sell eTBs through your stockbroker.

The face value of a Treasury Bond is $100. The coupon rate is set when the bond is first issued by the Commonwealth Government, it remains fixed for the life of the bond, and it is paid in instalments every six months. For example, a 5 percent Treasury Bond will pay interest of $2.50 every six months. The $100 face value is paid at maturity.

Exchange-traded Treasury Indexed Bonds

Exchange-traded Treasury Indexed Bonds (eTIBs) are also a convenient and easily accessible way to invest in Australian Government Treasury Indexed Bonds. An eTIB holder has beneficial ownership of Australian Government Treasury Indexed Bonds in the form of CHESS Depository Interests (CDIs) over which the eTIBs have been issued. There is a range of eTIBs available, and you will find them quoted on the ASX website. You can buy and sell eTIBs through your stockbroker.

The important difference is that an *indexed* bond provides protection against inflation. The face value of a Treasury Indexed Bond is $100 when it is first issued. The coupon rate on a Treasury Indexed Bond is set when the bond is first issued by the Commonwealth Government, and it is paid in instalments every three months. Both the coupon payments and the capital value payable at maturity increase in line with changes in the Consumer Price Index.

CORPORATE FIXED INCOME SECURITIES

In addition to borrowing money from financial institutions, companies also borrow money by issuing fixed income securities. Examples of corporate fixed income securities include fixed rate bonds, floating rate notes, and inflation-linked bonds. The market for company fixed income securities tends to be dominated by banks and other financial institutions which have a high credit rating. They issue large quantities of bonds, and their lines of debt are liquid and easily tradeable.

Corporate bonds, sometimes called *debentures*, are borrowings that are either secured by a fixed charge over specific assets of the company or a floating charge over the unpledged assets of the company. They are generally issued in units of $100 face value and pay interest half-yearly. The yields on company bonds are higher than for Commonwealth securities because they represent added risk. A trust deed provides for the appointment of a trustee to protect the bond holders' interests. Some company bond issues are listed on the ASX, but most are traded in the unlisted market.

Unsecured notes are also corporate borrowings that are generally issued in units of $100 face value. They tend to have a shorter maturity than bonds. Unsecured notes are also covered by a trust deed that is administered by an independent trustee, but they are not secured by a charge over any of the company's assets. If the company is ever wound up, unsecured note holders rank behind the bond holders and consequently offer a higher yield as compensation. Some unsecured notes are listed on the ASX, but most are traded in the unlisted market.

Most corporate fixed income securities are traded by institutions in the unlisted market that excludes direct access by private investors. There are a small number of corporate fixed income securities that are listed on the ASX which private investors can buy and sell through their stockbroker. Private investors can invest in corporate fixed income securities indirectly through units in exchange traded funds (ETFs) or through managed funds that specialise in fixed income securities. For investors with a relatively small portfolio, they are an excellent way to access a diversified portfolio of both listed and unlisted corporate fixed income securities.

HYBRID SECURITIES

Hybrid securities possess both debt and equity characteristics and the features can differ between individual issues. Hybrid securities generally pay a predetermined fixed or floating rate of interest. Unlike most other fixed income securities, hybrids may be callable, redeemable, or convertible into the company's ordinary shares. Hybrid securities are usually ranked behind other fixed income securities in the event of default. In recent years, hybrids have been popular due to higher yields and the ease in which private investors can trade them.

An example of a hybrid security is a convertible note. These are corporate unsecured notes that are convertible into the company's ordinary shares under certain conditions. They combine the advantages of a fixed interest security with the benefits of the ordinary share into which they may be converted. Convertible notes are generally listed on the ASX with the underlying company shares.

EXPECTED YIELD

An investor in a fixed income security knows in advance the face value and the coupon rate. Interest may be paid half-yearly or quarterly. The face value and the coupon rate are contractual obligations of the issuer that do not change. The market price of a fixed income security, however, will vary inversely with changes in the market rate of interest. Variations in the price of a fixed income security affect its expected rate of return or its expected *yield*. The concept of yield is critical to understanding fixed income securities. There are several ways to determine yield. We shall focus on the current yield, the yield to maturity, and the discount yield. They are easily calculated using the financial functions in an Excel spreadsheet.

Current yield

The current yield is the amount of the annual interest payments that a fixed income security provides in relation to its current market price. It is to a fixed income security what the dividend yield is to a share. It is the simplest way to measure yield, but its usefulness is somewhat limited. The current yield changes whenever the market price changes.

For example, a bond has a face value of $100, a coupon rate of 10 percent and 10 years term to maturity. If the market price is exactly $100, then the coupon rate and the current yield are equal at 10 percent. If the market price for the same bond is $80, then it is selling at a *discount* and the current yield is 12.5 percent. Alternatively, if the market price for the bond is $120, then it is selling at a *premium* and the current yield is 8.33 percent.

Yield to maturity

The yield to maturity is more useful for comparing the yields of fixed income securities with different prices, different coupon rates, and different terms to maturity. It reflects the effect of a premium or discount and it incorporates the compounding (reinvestment) effect of the interest payments over the life of a fixed income security. It assumes that it will be held to maturity and the interest payments will be reinvested at the same rate as the yield to maturity. If a bond with a face value of $100, a coupon rate of 10 percent and 10 years term to maturity is selling for $80, then the yield to maturity is 13.33 percent. It is greater than the equivalent current yield because it fully incorporates the recovery of the $20 discount in the market price. If the market price for the bond is $120, then the yield to maturity is 7.27 percent. Yield to maturity is lower than the equivalent current yield because it fully incorporates the loss of the $20 premium in the market price.

Discount yield

Discount securities do not make periodic interest payments but are sold at a discount from face value. They are generally quoted in terms of their discount yield. For example, a $100 face value Commonwealth Treasury Note that matures in 73 days and is currently selling for $98.81 has a discount yield of 6.0 percent per annum.

RISK IN FIXED INCOME SECURITIES

Compared with shares, fixed income securities are generally a lower risk. Nevertheless, every fixed income security carries some degree of risk. These include interest rate risk, reinvestment risk, inflation risk, credit risk, market liquidity risk, and sometimes call risk.

Interest rate risk

The price of a fixed income security varies inversely with changes in the market rate of interest. Therefore, rising market interest rates result in lower prices for fixed income securities and falling market interest rates result in higher prices for fixed income securities. You can suffer a capital loss if market rates of interest go up and you need to sell your fixed income securities before they mature. If market rates of interest go down, however, your fixed income securities will increase in price resulting in a capital gain if you sell before maturity. Interest rate risk is reflected in price volatility. Figure 11.1 illustrates the effect of a change in the market rate of interest on the price of a $100 face value bond with a 10 percent coupon rate and a ten year term to maturity.

Figure 11.1 Interest rate risk
Bond Prices
$100 face value, 10 percent coupon rate

	Market Rate of Interest		
Year	9 percent	10 percent	11 percent
1	106.00	100.00	94.46
2	105.53	100.00	94.85
3	105.03	100.00	95.29
4	104.49	100.00	95.77

(Continued)

Market Rate of Interest

Year	9 percent	10 percent	11 percent
5	103.89	100.00	96.30
6	103.24	100.00	96.90
7	102.53	100.00	97.56
8	101.76	100.00	98.29
9	100.92	100.00	99.10
10	100.00	100.00	100.00

As long as the market rate of interest remains at 10 percent, the bond will remain priced at $100 until it matures. If the market rate of interest falls to 9 percent the price of the bond will rise to $106.00. If the market rate of interest remains at 9 percent, the price of the bond will gradually decline each year until it reaches $100 face value at maturity. If the market rate of interest rises to 11 percent the price of the bond will fall to $94.46. If the market rate of interest remains at 11 percent, the price of the bond will gradually increase each year until it reaches $100 face value at maturity.

Interest rate risk also affects the reinvestment of interest payments. When interest payments are received, they are normally reinvested unless the funds are required for some other purpose. If the market rate of interest goes down, then the interest payments will be reinvested at the lower rate. If the market rate of interest goes up, then the interest payments will be reinvested at the higher rate. Figure 11.2 illustrates the effects of reinvestment risk using the same bond with a $100 face value, a 10 percent coupon rate and a 10 year term to maturity.

Figure 11.2 Reinvestment risk
Accumulated Interest Payments
$100 face value, 10 percent coupon rate

Reinvestment Rate

Year	9 percent	10 percent	11 percent
1	10.00	10.00	10.00
2	20.90	21.00	21.10
3	32.78	33.10	33.42
4	45.73	46.41	47.10
5	59.85	61.05	62.28
6	75.23	77.16	79.13
7	92.00	94.87	97.83
8	110.28	114.36	118.59
9	130.21	135.79	141.64
10	151.93	159.37	167.22

If the market rate of interest remains at 10 percent, the interest payments will be reinvested at 10 percent and interest earnings of $159.37 will accumulate by maturity. If the market rate of interest falls to 9 percent and remains at that level, the interest payments will be reinvested at 9 percent and interest earnings of $151.93 will accumulate by maturity. If the market rate of interest rises to 11 percent and remains at that level, the interest payments will be reinvested at 11 percent and interest earnings of $167.22 will accumulate by maturity.

Inflation risk

Inflation risk refers to the purchasing power of future interest and principal payments. When the rate of inflation is expected to rise, the prices of fixed income securities fall because the purchasing power of future interest and principal payments is diminished. Conversely, the prices of fixed income securities react favourably to a low rate of inflation. Fixed income securities are not usually a good hedge against inflation. If you are worried about inflation, you may want to consider indexed bonds in which the principal and/or the interest payments are adjusted according to movements in the Consumer Price Index.

Credit and default risk

Credit risk refers to the ability of the issuer to make the interest payments and to repay the face value at maturity. Commonwealth securities carry virtually no risk of default. Corporate credit risks vary according to financial structure, profitability, cash flow management, and the reliability of accounting practices. Standard and Poor's, Moody's and Fitch are credit rating agencies that assess the credit risk of fixed income securities. They make an objective evaluation of a fixed income security and assign a rating to reflect their assessment.

Fixed income securities with higher credit ratings generally have lower yields reflecting lower credit risk. Those with lower credit ratings generally have higher yields reflecting greater credit risk. If an issuer's credit risk increases, then their credit rating may be downgraded. Investors will react to a lower credit rating by demanding a greater yield to compensate for the increased risk. A greater yield can only be achieved by driving down the price.

Market liquidity risk

Market liquidity risk means that a fixed income security may be difficult to resell once you own it. This can be the result of too few buyers and sellers so that trading is infrequent or sporadic. The greater the market liquidity risk, the greater the required yield and the lower the market price. Exchange-traded Government bonds, most ASX listed company fixed income securities, and Exchange Traded Funds carry little liquidity risk compared with equivalent securities traded in the unlisted market.

Call risk

Call risk only applies to fixed income securities with a call provision. A call provision means that the issuer can repurchase the securities from investors before the maturity date at a specified price. For example, if market interest rates go below the coupon rate on a bond issue, then the company may decide to call the bonds and issue new ones with a lower coupon rate. It is traditional for the call price to consist of face value plus a premium equivalent to one year's interest. Call risk means you could be forced to liquidate a high-yielding investment. Call risk is greatest when interest rates are high and expected to fall. When interest rates are expected to rise, yield differentials for call risk are negligible.

MARKET INTEREST RATES

The main reason that the prices of fixed income securities fluctuate is due to changes in the market rate of interest. Yields on individual fixed income securities are sometimes affected by the credit risk of the borrower, the liquidity of the secondary market and the term to maturity, but they are always tied together by changes in the overall market rate of interest. Inasmuch as the Reserve Bank has considerable influence over interest rates through monetary policy, any expected changes in those policies will affect the market prices for fixed income securities. Despite attempts to forecast the direction and magnitude of movements in interest rates, many of the economic and political variables that affect interest rates are difficult to predict. Getting a grip on the nature of interest rates means understanding the significance of the yield curve, how changes to interest rates occur, and how the changes affect the price volatility of fixed income securities.

A *yield curve* relates the yields for fixed income securities that are comparable in all respects except their term to maturity. The yield curve is a snapshot of the *term structure* of interest rates at a point in time and it can be used to anticipate the effects of changes in interest rates on the prices of fixed income securities. Figure 11.3 is an example to two different kinds of yield curves.

The normal or ascending yield curve consists of rising yields as maturities become longer. It is the most common shape of the yield curve, and it tends to prevail when market interest rates are moderate or low. Generally, the longer the maturity, the higher the yield because there is more uncertainty about potential long-term changes to interest rates, inflation, and the credit risk of the issuers.

The descending yield curve consists of falling yields as maturities become longer. It is not very common and tends to occur when short-term market interest rates are relatively high. The descending yield curve is strong evidence of intervention by the Reserve Bank. The slope of the yield curve usually flattens out for longer maturities so that yield differentials become insignificant

Figure 11.3 Yield curves

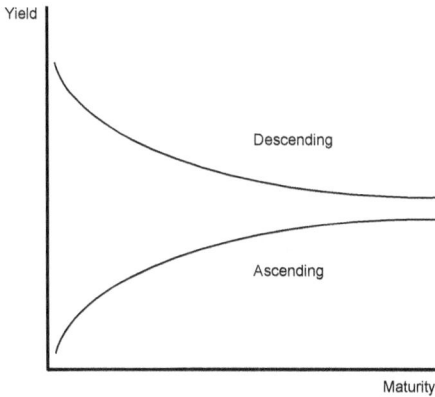

When the term structure of interest rates changes the yield curve is not only capable of shifting up and down, but it can also change shape. Short-term interest rates are essentially the Reserve Bank's monetary policy instrument for controlling liquidity in the economy. The cost of short-term funds forms the foundation of the interest rate structure that flows through to the cost of longer-term fixed income securities. A neutral or loose monetary policy results in an ascending yield curve, and a tight monetary policy results in a descending yield curve.

Longer-term interest rates tend to float more freely according to the supply and demand for long-term funds and the expectations for inflation. Long-term funds are needed by the Commonwealth, state governments, local governments, and the corporate sector. The sources of long-term funds are the domestic household sector and overseas lenders. Therefore, anything that affects the supply and demand for long-term funds will affect long-term interest rates. Expectations are probably more important than actual changes in explaining the day-to-day volatility of long-term interest rates.

A change in the market rate of interest will result in greater price volatility to the extent that maturity is longer, the coupon rate is lower, and the market rate of interest from which a change begins is higher. Conversely, a change in the market rate of interest will result in less price volatility to the extent that maturity is shorter, the coupon rate is higher, and the market rate of interest from which a change begins is lower. The practical implications of these principles are important when it comes to making investment decisions in fixed income securities. If you are trying to maximise capital gains from falling market interest rates, look for high price-volatility fixed income securities that have long maturities and low coupon rates. If you are trying to minimise capital losses from rising market interest rates, look for low price-volatility fixed income securities that have short maturities and high coupon rates.

SUMMARY

Fixed income securities are sometimes called debt securities, interest rate securities, bonds, debentures, or notes. They can be issued by the Commonwealth government, state governments, semi-government agencies and companies. They vary in terms of the issuer, risk, return, marketability, maturity, and the frequency of interest payments. The return on a fixed income security is its yield. There are different ways to calculate yield including the current yield, the yield to maturity, and the discount yield. Compared with shares, fixed income securities are generally a lower risk. Nevertheless, every fixed income security carries some degree of risk including interest rate risk, reinvestment risk, inflation risk, credit risk, market liquidity risk, and sometimes call risk. The main reason that the prices of fixed income securities fluctuate is due to changes in the market rate of interest. The yield curve is a snapshot of the term structure of interest rates at a point in time and it can be used to anticipate the effects of changes in the market rate of interest on the prices of fixed income securities.

CHAPTER 12

FIXED INCOME INVESTMENT STRATEGIES

Conservative investors have traditionally regarded fixed income securities as a source of steady income. In most cases the risk is small and with Commonwealth government issues there is no practical risk of default. These investors tend to use a simple buy-and-hold strategy. Other investors seeking somewhat higher returns will try to maximise their yield subject to whatever risk they are willing to bear. Corporate issues return more than government issues, BBB ratings return more than AAA ratings and longer maturities generally return more than shorter maturities. Although most conservative investors plan to hold their investments until maturity, they need to consider the consequences if conditions change and they must sell out early.

Investment strategies for fixed income securities range from simple to sophisticated. Some are easy to manage while others require day-to-day monitoring and supervision. First, we examine the impact of inflation and taxes on the real rate of return from investments in fixed income securities. Next, we look at several passive and active investment strategies including a technique known as *duration*. Last, we consider the opportunities available with convertible notes.

INFLATION AND TAXES

The yield to maturity is the expected rate of return from an investment in a fixed income security. Inflation and taxes, however, erode the yield to maturity. If an investment in a fixed income security earns 4 percent and your marginal tax rate is 45 percent, then your after-tax return is only 2.2 percent. If annual inflation is more than 2.2 percent, then your real return after tax is **negative.** That is why the prices of long-term fixed income securities decline when inflation rises to make the yield more attractive.

The danger of inflation is not recognising the loss of purchasing power. For example, an investor buys long-term fixed income securities on the assumption that the fixed income will provide a comfortable retirement. However, after a few years it turns out that the fixed income is no longer able to support the investor's requirements. The solution is to avoid extremely long-term investments and to diversify the maturities of different investments. This gives you flexibility and helps to avoid the lost opportunities that plague fixed interest investors.

The first goal of investing is to keep pace with inflation on an after-tax basis. You can calculate the breakeven interest rate by dividing the expected inflation rate by 100 percent minus your tax rate. For example, if you are on the 45 percent tax rate and you expect the inflation rate to average about 3 percent, then your breakeven yield is 5.45 percent.

$$\text{Breakeven yield} = \frac{\text{Expected inflation rate}}{100 \text{ percent} - \text{Tax rate}} = \frac{3 \text{ percent}}{100 \text{ percent} - 45 \text{ percent}} = 5.45 \text{ percent}$$

In extreme circumstances, you may need to choose between seeking a high-risk breakeven yield or simply minimising the loss to your spending power. Minimising the loss to your spending power is sometimes a better alternative than risking the loss of your principal.

PASSIVE STRATEGIES

Passive investment strategies in fixed income securities are characterised by the fact that they make no judgement about future interest rates. Passive investors are generally long-term investors who are not actively seeking to improve their returns beyond the market yield. Passive investment strategies consist of buy-and-hold and laddering.

Buy and hold

An investor who buys a fixed income security with the intention of holding it until maturity can look forward to four possible types of returns.

- Interest payments.
- Reinvestment of the interest payments.
- A capital gain if it was bought at a discount from face value.
- A capital loss if it was bought at a premium from face value.

A buy-and-hold strategy simply consists of buying fixed income securities that meet the investor's investment criteria and holding them until they mature. Short-term cash flow requirements can be invested in short-term securities and long-term cash flow requirements can be matched with longer-term maturities. A buy-and-hold strategy minimises interest rate risk, but it does not protect the investor from other forms of risk. Figure 12.1 illustrates the buy-and-hold results of investing in a bond with a $100 face value, 10 percent coupon and a 10-year term to maturity. If the market rate of interest remains at 10 percent, then the total compound value at the end of Year 10 is $259.37.

Figure 12.1 Investment results at 10 percent

Year	Interest	Price	Total	Percent Return
1	10.00	100.00	110.00	10
2	21.00	100.00	121.00	10
3	33.10	100.00	133.10	10
4	46.41	100.00	146.41	10
5	61.05	100.00	161.05	10
6	77.16	100.00	177.16	10
7	94.87	100.00	194.87	10
8	114.36	100.00	214.36	10
9	135.79	100.00	235.79	10
10	159.37	100.00	259.37	10

Figure 12.2 illustrates the investment results if the market rate of interest falls to 9 percent in the first year and remains there until maturity. The increase in price lifts returns in the early years which more than compensates for the reduction in the reinvestment rate. However, a buy-and-hold strategy does not take advantage of the capital gain in Year 1 and the total compound value of the investment at the end of Year 10 is a bit lower at $251.93.

Figure 12.2 Investment results at 9 percent

Year	Interest	Price	Total	Percent Return
1	10.00	106.00	116.00	16.00
2	20.90	105.53	126.43	12.44
3	32.78	105.03	137.81	11.28
4	45.73	104.49	150.22	10.71
5	59.85	103.89	163.74	10.36
6	75.23	103.24	178.47	10.14
7	92.00	102.53	194.54	9.97
8	110.28	101.76	212.04	9.85
9	130.21	100.92	231.13	9.76
10	151.93	100.00	251.93	9.68

Figure 12.3 illustrates the investment results if the market rate of interest rises to 11 percent in the first year and remains there until maturity. The decrease in price depresses returns in the early years until the increased reinvestment rate compensates for it. A buy-and-hold strategy would avoid the capital loss in the early years and the total compound value at the end of Year 10 is lifted to $267.22.

Figure 12.3 Investment results at 11 percent

Year	Interest	Price	Total	Percent Return
1	10.00	94.46	104.46	4.46
2	21.10	94.85	115.95	7.68
3	33.42	95.29	128.71	8.78
4	47.10	95.77	142.87	9.33
5	62.28	96.30	158.58	9.66
6	79.13	96.90	176.03	9.88
7	97.83	97.56	195.39	10.04
8	118.59	98.29	216.88	10.16
9	141.64	99.10	240.74	10.25
10	167.22	100.00	267.22	10.33

Laddering

If you choose maturities that are very long, you will generally get higher yields. But you also run the risk of loss of principle if market interest rates rise, prices decline, and you need to sell before maturity. If you choose maturities that are very short, you can preserve your principal but you will generally get lower yields.

Another strategy for protecting against interest rate risk is to *ladder* your maturities. This consists of placing equal investments into evenly spaced maturities. Not only will the returns be an average between the short-term and long-term yields, but also an average of market yields over time. Proceeds from interest payments and maturing securities are reinvested in longer-dated securities to maintain the laddering of maturities. Laddering also offers greater liquidity than a buy-and-hold strategy because a portion of the portfolio is always maturing. An alternative form of the laddering strategy is to use one short-term maturity and one long-term maturity. By eliminating intermediate-term maturities, you obtain increased liquidity from the short-dated securities and increased returns from the long-dated securities.

ACTIVE STRATEGIES

Active strategies are characterised by making forecasts about future interest rates and using these forecasts to produce additional returns. Active strategies are also higher-risk strategies because interest rate forecasting is a notoriously difficult task. These are generally short-term strategies that require continual monitoring and more frequent trading. An example of an active investment strategy is called 'riding the yield curve'.

We introduced the yield curve in Chapter 11. It depicts changes in the yield to maturity from short-term securities to long-term securities that are identical in all other respects. A normal yield curve slopes upward as the term to maturity increases reflecting higher yields on longer-term securities. If the yield curve remains normal, we can increase the returns on short-term investments by riding the yield curve. This strategy consists of buying fixed income securities further out on the yield curve, riding them down the slope, and then rolling them over again. For example, buying bonds with 180 days to maturity and selling them when they have 90 days left to maturity will result in a better return than holding them to maturity. Riding the yield curve with minimum risk means you need to be able to hold on until maturity if market interest rates change and the yield curve shifts position. For the investor who wants to speculate on changes in market interest rates there are more aggressive strategies such as the interest rate futures contracts discussed in Chapter 10.

DURATION

Duration is an important technique because it provides a convenient summary of the three key variables that determine price movements in fixed income securities. They are the coupon rate, the time to maturity and the level of market interest rates. Duration not only enables you to determine the holding period for which interest rate risk and reinvestment risk are virtually eliminated, but you can also compare the price sensitivity of different fixed income securities by comparing their duration. For these reasons, duration has assumed an important role in managing debt investments. Figure 12.4 plots the yearly percent returns from Figures 12.1, 12.2 and 12.3 over the 10-year life of the bond.

Figure 12.4 Duration point

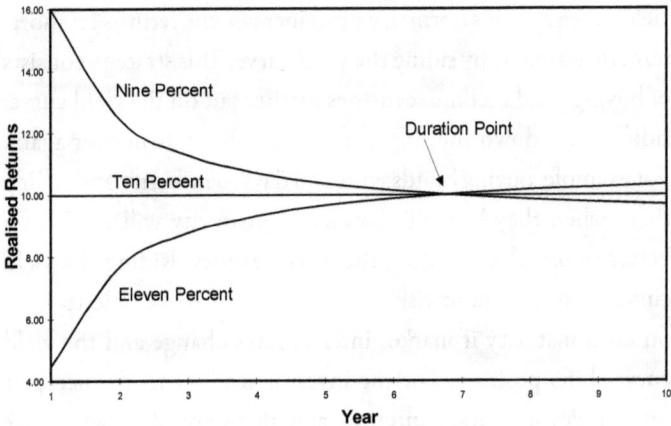

If the market rate of interest remains at 10 percent, then the yearly returns are constant. If the market rate of interest drops to 9 percent, then the yearly returns are highest in Year 1 declining to the lowest in Year 10. If the market rate of interest increases to 11 percent, then the yearly returns are lowest in Year 1 rising to the highest in Year 10. At a point in time the three lines converge. This is known as the *duration point*. It is the investment horizon in which the future value of a fixed income security and its reinvested interest payments are unaffected by changes in the market rate of interest. The duration point can be calculated using the financial functions in an Excel spreadsheet.

The duration point in this example is 6.759 years. It tells an investor two things. First, a duration of 6.759 years means if you hold this bond for about 6 years and 9 months, you can virtually eliminate interest rate risk. Second, a duration of 6.759 means that for every 1 percent change in the market rate of interest, the bond price will change in the opposite direction by approximately 6.759 percent. It is a measure of the bond's price volatility because of changes in the market rate of interest.

If the holding period for a fixed income security is equal to its duration, it is said to be *immunised*. Immunisation means that its realised rate of return will be equal to its expected rate of return regardless of any changes in the market rate of interest. An investor with a definite investment time horizon can minimise interest rate risk by holding a fixed income security with a duration equal to the time horizon. Duration can also be calculated for a portfolio of fixed income securities.

Duration gives an investor the means to obtain the minimum interest rate risk for a portfolio of fixed income securities with a given set of investment objectives. This is the baseline portfolio that is fully immunised as a result of having a duration equal to the planned investment horizon. If the investor wants to try to forecast the future shape and level of the yield curve, they can engage in active investment strategies that alter the baseline portfolio to improve the rate of return.

If interest rates are expected to rise, overall duration can be shortened to reduce the effect of an expected fall in fixed income security prices and take advantage of improved reinvestment income. If interest rates are expected to fall, overall duration can be lengthened to reduce the effect of lower reinvestment income and take advantage of increases in fixed income security prices. The further an investor departs from the baseline portfolio, however, the more interest rate risk they incur.

Duration also provides an approximate measure of price volatility. A decrease in the market rate of interest will have the opposite effect on the price. The longer the duration, the more volatile will be the price movement. In other words, there is a direct relationship between duration and interest rate risk. This relationship between duration and interest rate risk is the key to active investment strategies by shaping a portfolio with maximum price sensitivity during declining interest rates and minimum price sensitivity during rising interest rates. Duration does this with a great deal more precision than simply relying upon the term to maturity.

CONVERTIBLE NOTES

Convertible notes are corporate fixed income securities that can be converted into ordinary shares. Convertible note holders have the right, but not the obligation, to convert their notes to ordinary shares on specified dates or during a specified period. If the notes are not converted they are repaid at face value on the maturity date.

Convertible notes are generally unsecured and the yield is somewhat lower than an equivalent note that is not convertible because the conversion privilege has value. The distinguishing feature of the note is a conversion ratio that specifies the number of shares into which the note may be converted. If the market rate of interest is greater than the coupon rate, then the convertible note will trade at a discount from its face value. If the market rate of interest is less than the coupon rate, then the convertible note will trade at a premium over its face value.

However, if the market price of the ordinary shares becomes greater than the conversion price, then the convertible note will be valued according to the market price of the underlying ordinary shares.

Convertible note holders have the upside opportunity to participate in any capital appreciation that may take place in the shares. At the same time, they have the downside protection of being creditors if the company should encounter hard times. In the meantime, they are entitled to receive regular fixed interest payments. For these reasons, the analysis of a convertible note not only includes consideration of its characteristics as a fixed income security, but also the valuation of the underlying ordinary shares.

Most convertible notes are exchangeable into the underlying shares at a fixed rate during the life of the note. However, this rate may change because of a share split, a bonus issue, a takeover or other circumstances. The conversion privilege may also expire before the note matures or it may not be effective until sometime after it is issued. Sometimes the conversion ratio declines at regular intervals.

SUMMARY

Investment strategies for fixed income securities range from simple to sophisticated. Some are easy to manage while others require day-to-day monitoring and supervision. Inflation and taxes reduce the real rate of return from an investment in fixed income securities and we calculate the minimum yield necessary to break even.

Passive investment strategies are characterised by the fact that they make no judgement about future interest rates. They consist of buy and hold and laddering.

Active investment strategies are characterised by making forecasts about interest rates and using them to produce additional returns. They consist of riding the yield curve and employing a sophisticated technique known as duration.

The chapter concludes with a description of the opportunities available by investing in convertible notes.

GLOSSARY

Abnormal items Large gains or losses in a company's income statement that do not occur in the normal course of business.

Accumulation index A share price index that assumes dividends and interest are reinvested.

Active portfolio management A style of investment management that seeks higher returns. Opposite of *passive* investment management.

American-style option An option that may be exercised at any time.

Arbitrage Buying and selling equivalent securities at the same time in different markets in order to profit from a difference in price.

Ask price The lowest price that sellers are willing to accept, also called the *offer* price.

Asset allocation The systematic placement of funds into various classes of securities in a portfolio.

ASX A commonly used abbreviation for the Australian Securities Exchange.

At best An instruction to buy or sell at the broker's discretion as to price, also called *at discretion*.

At-the-money When the exercise price of an option is equal to the market price of the underlying asset.

Australian Securities and Investment Commission (ASIC) The government corporate regulatory body for the securities markets.

Authorised capital The amount of share capital with which a company is registered.

Averaging down Buying more of a security as its price falls.

Bank accepted bill (BAB) A negotiable discount fixed income security with a typical maturity of 90 or 180 days that is guaranteed by a bank.

Basis point One-hundredth of one percent, the minimum unit of movement in interest rates.

Bear Someone who expects prices to decline. A *bear market* is a period of generally declining prices.

Benchmark An index or other measurement used to assess the risk and performance of a portfolio.

Beta factor A measurement of a security's volatility relative to the volatility of the market.

Bid-ask spread The difference between the bid price and the ask price.

Bid price The highest price that buyers are willing to pay.

Blue chip Shares in a leading company that are considered to be of high quality.

Board (of directors) A group of individuals elected by shareholders to formulate and direct a company's policies and objectives.

Bond See *fixed income security*.

Bonus issue Distribution of additional shares without charge on a pro rata basis to existing shareholders.

Book value The value of assets in the company's books of account.

Books closing date The date on which a company closes its share registry to determine the shareholders who are entitled to a dividend, bonus issue or rights issue.

Bottom (out) The lowest price before the reversal of a downtrend.

Bourse The French word for stock exchange.

Breakout A price rise above a resistance level or a price decline below a support level.

Broker See *stockbroker*.

Brokerage commission Fee charged by a stockbroker for transacting securities on behalf of a client.

Bull Someone who expects prices to rise. A *bull market* is a period of generally rising prices.

Business cycle The boom and bust pattern of economic activity.

Call option The right to buy a certain number of securities at a fixed price within a specific period of time.

Call provision A feature of some fixed income securities in which they may be retired or redeemed by the company before maturity.

Capital The funds invested in a company. Similarly, the funds an individual or fund manager has available to invest in securities.

Capital gain (loss) The difference between the price paid for a security and the price received when it is sold.

Capital structure The relative proportions of debt and equity capital in a company's balance sheet.

Capitalisation See *market capitalisation*.

Cash management trust A unit trust that invests in short-term money market securities.

Cash rate The current interest rate in the short-term money market.

Charting See *technical analysis*.

CHESS The ASX *Clearing House Electronic Subregister System* that is used to transfer listed shareholdings electronically.

Churning Excessive trading.

Class of options Options of the same type (call or put) and style (American or European) over the same underlying security.

Client adviser A licensed individual that is employed by a stockbroker to advise clients and accept orders.

Close out To offset a currently held position.

Closed-end fund A fund that no longer accepts new investments. Opposite of *open-end fund*.

Congestion When the price of a security fluctuates within a narrow range.

Consolidated accounts Financial statement for a group of companies owned by a parent company.

Contract note A document sent to a buyer or seller by a stockbroker confirming that a transaction has been completed.

Contributing share Ordinary shares that are not fully paid up.

Convertible Fixed interest securities or preference shares that can be converted into ordinary shares.

Correction A price decline after a period of rising prices, the opposite of a *rally*.

Coupon rate The rate of interest on a fixed interest security stated as a percentage of its par value.

Cover Cash or securities lodged by a client with their broker when buying on margin. Also, to close out a short position.

Covered option writing Selling options while owning the underlying security.

Cum dividend Shares that are trading with the buyer entitled to the declared dividend (trading *with* the dividend).

Cum rights Shares that are trading with the buyer entitled to the rights issue then current (trading *with* the rights).

Cumulative A provision in some preference shares in which passed dividends are accumulated and payable before any ordinary dividends may be paid.

CXA The abbreviation for the Chi-X securities exchange.

Day only An order that is cancelled at the end of the day if it is not executed.

Day trader Someone who buys and sells in the same day.

Dealer A person who has a licence issued by the Australian Securities and Investments Commission to place orders to buy and sell securities.

Debenture A fixed interest security issued by a company and secured by a floating charge over all of its unpledged assets.

Delist Removal of a security from trading on an exchange.

Delivery month The month in which a futures contract expires.

Derivative A security that represents a claim on an underlying asset, such as options and futures contracts.

Discount The amount by which a security is quoted below its face or par value, the opposite of *premium*.

Discretionary account An agreement in which a client gives a broker the authority to trade the client's account.

Diversification Spreading a portfolio over a number of securities with the objective of reducing risk, see also *asset allocation*.

Dividend The part of company profits that is distributed to shareholders.

Dividend imputation A tax credit attached to a dividend, known as a *franking credit*, for the company tax that has already been paid on the company's profits.

Dividend reinvestment plan A scheme whereby shareholders can elect to receive their dividends in shares, usually at a discount from the current market price, rather than in cash.

Dividend yield Annual dividends per share divided by the current share price.

Duration The investment horizon for a fixed income security in which interest rate risk is eliminated.

Earnings per share (EPS) Net profit after tax divided by the number of ordinary shares.

Entry price The price at which a unit in a unit trust is issued, also known as *purchase price*.

Equity security Ownership in a company evidenced by shares.

Equity option See *option*.

Equity trust A managed fund that invests in shares.

European-style option An option that may only be exercised when it expires.

Ex dividend Shares trading with the seller entitled to the declared dividend (trading *without* the dividend).

Ex dividend date The date when shares change from being quoted *cum* dividend to *ex* dividend.

Ex rights Shares trading with the seller entitled to the rights issue then current (selling *without* the rights).

Ex rights date The date when shares change from being quoted *cum* rights to *ex* rights.

Exchange traded option See *option*.

Execute Completion of a transaction or a trade.

Exercise To invoke the right to buy or sell the underlying security conferred by an option.

Exercise price The price at which an option can be exercised, also known as the *strike* price.

Expiry date The date on which an option or futures contract expires.

Extraordinary item A gain or loss in a company's income statement not usually associated with the normal activities of the company.

Face value The nominal or stated value of a fixed income security indicating the principal amount to be repaid at maturity.

Final dividend a dividend paid after the end of a company's financial year.

Financial futures A futures contract in which the underlying asset is a financial security.

Financial structure Relative proportions of debt and equity in a company's balance sheet.

Fintech The integration of technology into offerings by financial services companies.

Fixed income security Loan securities, such as bank accepted bills, Commonwealth notes and bonds, debentures and unsecured notes.

Float Raising capital for a company by public subscription.

Franking credit See *dividend imputation*.

Front-end load A fee paid to buy into a unit trust.

Fund manager A professional investment manager.

Fundamental analysis An attempt to determine the fair value of a security.

Futures contract A standardised contract to buy or sell an underlying asset at a price agreed to today for delivery in the future.

Gearing The proportion of debt capital in a company's capital structure, also called *leverage*.

Gilt-edged Fixed interest securities that are considered to be of good quality.

Good 'till cancelled (GTC) An order that remains until it is executed or cancelled.

Hedge A transaction that protects against unwanted price movements.

Holder The buyer of an options contract, the opposite of *writer*.

Holder Identification Number (HIN) Used to identify the owner of shares sponsored by a stockbroker.

Hybrid security A security that combines elements of fixed income securities and equity securities.

Imputation See *dividend imputation*.

Index A number series used to measure broad changes in the price of securities.

Index warrant A warrant covering one of the prescribed indices of the Australian Securities Exchange.

Index bond A Treasury bond that can be *capital* indexed and/or *interest* indexed according to changes in the Consumer Price Index.

Index fund A managed fund that tracks an index.

Initial public offering (IPO) The first public sale of securities. See *float*.

Inside information Confidential information that is only available to a small number of people. Trading on the basis of inside information (*insider trading*) is illegal.

Institutional investor An organisation employing professional investment managers such as life insurance companies, banks and unit trusts.

Intangible asset An asset that has no tangible or material form such as goodwill or trademarks.

Interim dividend A dividend paid after the first half of a company's financial year.

Interim report A report on company operations for the first half of the financial year.

In-the-money An option with intrinsic value.

Intrinsic value A positive difference between the price of an option's underlying asset and the exercise price.

Issued capital The amount of a company's authorised capital that has been issued to shareholders.

GLOSSARY

Joint venture An agreement in which two or more parties jointly explore, finance, operate or invest in a venture.

Junk bonds Low-quality, high-risk fixed interest securities.

LEPO Low exercise price option.

Leverage The process of increasing the funds available for investment by borrowing.

Limit order An instruction placing a limit on the highest price to be paid or the lowest price at which to sell.

Limited liability (Ltd) When an investor's liability is limited to the fully paid value of the shares held.

Liquid market A market in which a security can be quickly and easily bought or sold. Opposite of a *thin* market.

Listed security A security that is traded on an exchange.

Loan to valuation ratio (LVR) The maximum amount of a margin loan.

Long (position) Owning a security, the opposite of *short* (position).

Margin Borrowing by a client in part payment for the purchase of securities. In futures trading, a good faith deposit required to be lodged when entering a contract.

Mark to market A *margin call* to settle margin variations as a result of adverse price movement.

Market capitalisation The value of a company found by multiplying the number of shares outstanding by the market price.

Market order An instruction to buy or sell immediately at the best price currently available.

Maturity The date on which a fixed interest security is due to be repaid.

Merger A friendly takeover.

Minority interest The value of profits and equity that is attributable to the holders of interests in subsidiaries that are not wholly owned.

Money market A market in which financial institutions trade short-term fixed income securities such as treasury notes and bank accepted bills.

Mortgage A pledge over an asset to secure a loan.

Negative gearing A tax reducing strategy in which the interest cost of borrowing exceeds the income earned from an investment.

Negotiable security A transferable security that can be bought or sold.

Net asset backing (NAB) Assets less liabilities divided by the number of shares outstanding.

Net asset value (NAV) Net asset backing per unit in a unit trust.

No liability (NL) Applied to some mining and oil company partly-paid shares in which a call for the unpaid portion cannot be enforced. However, failure to meet the call can result in forfeiture of the shares.

Nominal value See *face value.*

Note A fixed interest security.

NSX The abbreviation for the National Stock Exchange of Australia.

Offer price See *ask price.*

Off 'Change Transactions in listed securities that do not take place on an exchange.

Open-end fund A fund in which investors can buy and sell units at any time based on net asset value, the opposite of *closed-end fund.*

Open interest The number of outstanding derivative contracts for a particular class or series.

Open order An order that is good until it has been executed or cancelled.

Option The right to buy or sell an underlying asset on specified terms.

Ordinary shares Units of proportional ownership in a company.

Out-of-the-money An option with no intrinsic value.

Over-bought A recent price rise for which there is now an expected correction.

Over-sold A recent price decline for which there is now an expected rally.

Over-the-counter Trading via the telephone or computer screens that does not take place on an organised exchange.

Overweight Having greater exposure to an asset class than would be normal, the opposite of *underweight.*

Paper profit (or losses) Unrealised capital gains (or losses).

Par value See *face value.*

Pari passu A class of securities that has equal rights with another class of securities.

Partly-paid shares See *contributing shares.*

Passive portfolio management A style of buy-and-hold investment management, the opposite of *active portfolio management.*

Penny stocks Speculative low-priced shares, also called *penny dreadfuls.*

Play Jargon for a way to profit from an undervalued or overvalued situation.

Pooled investment Any form of investment in which individuals collectively place their funds with a professional investment manager.

Portfolio A selection of securities chosen according to an investor's goals.

Preference share Shares that have preferential rights over ordinary shares to dividends and assets.

Premium The amount by which a security is quoted above its face value, opposite of a *discount*. Also, the price paid for a put or call.

Price earnings ratio (P/E) Current share price divided by annual earnings per ordinary share.

Primary market When securities are first issued and the funds constitute new capital to the firm. See *secondary market*.

Private placement The sale of securities directly to an individual or institutional investor without being offered to the public.

Product disclosure statement Document or group of documents that contain information about a financial product.

Program trading Orders automatically triggered by a computer when certain conditions are present.

Property trust Pooled investments that specialise in real estate.

Prospectus A legal document issued by a company setting out the terms of its public issue of securities.

Proxy Written authorisation given by a shareholder for another person to vote their shares at a shareholders meeting.

Punter A speculator who buys and sells frequently.

Put option The right to sell a certain number of securities at a fixed price within a specific period of time.

Quotation Prices at which buyers and sellers are prepared to trade, see also *bid* and *ask*.

Rally A price rise after a period of declining prices, opposite of *correction*.

Ratings Indicators of the creditworthiness or riskiness of issuers of fixed interest securities.

Realised profit (or loss) A profit (or loss) resulting from the liquidation of an investment.

Resistance level A point at which an upward price movement is expected to slow down or stop.

Return Income and capital gains expressed as an annual percentage of the amount invested.

Rights issue A privilege granted to existing shareholders to buy new shares usually below the current market price.

Risk The chance that the realised rate of return will be different from the expected rate of return. See *volatility*.

Robo advisor Automated investment advice service

SEATS *Stock Exchange Automated Trading System*, the computer trading system used by the ASX.

Secondary market When existing (as opposed to new) securities are traded, also called the *aftermarket*. See *primary market*.

Secured Fixed income securities that are covered by pledged assets.

Securities Evidence of ownership of bonds, debentures, notes or shares.

Securityholder Reference Number (SRN) Used to identify the owner of shares sponsored through a company's share registry.

Semi-government bonds Fixed interest securities issued by State government owned authorities.

Series Options of the same class that have the same expiry and exercise price.

Settlement and transfer Delivery of cash from the buyer and securities from the seller to complete a transaction.

Share price index See *Index*.

Share register The record of a company's shareholders.

Shareholders' funds The amount of accumulated capital and reserves in a company's balance sheet.

Short (position) Selling securities that are not owned with the intention of buying them back (covering) later at a lower price, the opposite of *long* (position).

Speculator An individual who accepts high risks in an attempt to earn large profits.

Split Increasing a company's shares outstanding by distributing additional shares pro rata to shareholders.

Spread Buying or selling one security and simultaneously taking the opposite position in another.

Stag An investor who buys securities in a new issue with the intention of reselling them immediately at a profit.

Stock See *securities*.

Stock screener A computer tool that sorts through potential investments according to specified criteria.

Stockbroker A firm that buys and sells securities for clients.

Stockmarket Trading in all securities irrespective of whether they are traded on an exchange or over-the-counter.

Stop-loss order An instruction to sell if a security's price falls below a specified level.

Straddle Simultaneously buying and selling different derivatives.

Strap Two calls and a put.

Strike price See *exercise price.*

Strip Two puts and a call.

Subscribe To buy securities being offered for sale in a prospectus.

Subsidiary A company that is owned or controlled by another company.

Support level A point at which a downward price movement is expected to slow down or stop.

Sweetener A feature in a securities offering, such as convertibility, that encourages investors to subscribe.

Takeover The acquisition of a controlling interest in a company.

Technical analysis Predicting future price movements from an analysis of past price movements.

Time value The difference between an option premium and its intrinsic value.

Thin market Sporadic trading in a security caused by too few buyers and sellers resulting in exaggerated price swings when trades do take place.

Tick or Tic The minimum change in price. Used primarily in bond and futures trading.

Top (out) The highest price before the reversal of an uptrend.

Trader An investor who actively buys and sells securities over a relatively short time.

Treasury bond An interest bearing fixed income security issued by the Australian government.

Treasury note A discount fixed income security issued by the Australian government for maturities less than 12 months.

Trust See *unit trust.*

Trust Deed An agreement for the methods of receipt, investment and disbursement of funds.

Underlying asset The asset subject to being bought or sold upon exercise of an option or delivery on a futures contract.

Underwriter A financial institution that assists in the issue of new securities by agreeing to purchase any unsold securities thereby guaranteeing that they will be fully subscribed.

Unit trust An organisation that pools and manages investor's money by selling *units* in an investment trust.

Unlisted shares Trade in the over-the- counter market and not on an exchange.

Unsecured note A fixed interest security that is not secured by a mortgage or other charge over a company's assets.

Volume Number of securities traded.

Volatility Degree of variation in the price or returns of a security. Measured by the annualised standard deviation. Also, see *Beta*.

Warrant A long-dated option contract issued by a third party.

Whipsaw Frequent buy and sell signals within a narrow price range resulting in numerous small losses.

Winding up The dissolution of a company in which the assets are liquidated to satisfy the creditors before any remaining funds are returned to the shareholders.

Writer A seller of options, the opposite of *holder*.

Yield The annual income from a security (interest or dividend) expressed as a percentage of its current market price.

Yield curve A graph showing the relationship of yield to maturity and term to maturity for a group of similar fixed income securities.

Yield to maturity The average annual return from a fixed income security purchased at the current market price and held to maturity.

Zero coupon bond A fixed income security that pays no interest but is sold at a deep discount from face value.

INDEX

INDEX

www.ingramcontent.com/pod-product-compliance
Lightning Source LLC
Chambersburg PA
CBHW060548200326
41521CB00007B/524